she who OVERCOMES

RISING OUT Of The ASHES Of Your CIRCUMSTANCES

MANDY B. ANDERSON

PRAISE FOR *she who* OVERCOMES

"With every word and every story in *She Who Overcomes*, something familiar reawakened inside of me: A yearning to press beyond the "Why?" of what happens to us in life, to the "What Next?" of those circumstances or choices. Mandy reminds us that because we are children of God, we are called and equipped to overcome these times through courage, persistence and grace. She challenges the reader through thoughtful and meaningful questions, and she lovingly empowers you with tools that help you to begin rising out of your own ashes of life, whatever they may be. You know those books you start to read and you can't put down? This is one of those books—but it's also one that you will pick up again and again, and share with the women you care about most." **~Marci Narum, Speaker and Coach**

"For any woman who longs to live life to the fullest, this is a MUST read! Throughout the pages, you will find stories of hope that will fill your soul and give you the needed strength and courage to live life fully and to overcome the challenges and obstacles that can so easily hold us back! Mandy is one of the most inspirational women I know! Her authenticity shines through on the pages of her book and quite honestly, you will walk away knowing that you are not alone in this journey through life!" **~Dr. Jen Bennett, iBloom Social Media Specialist**

"With generous doses of humor, beautiful moments of truth, and a little tough love Mandy paints a picture of what life looks like when you wear the title of a *She Who Overcomes*. Based on God-breathed truths from the book of Revelation, and Mandy's inspiring testimony, *She Who Overcomes* will encourage you to live brave, authentic, and beautifully whole. This soul-stirring book will provide you with a roadmap to overcome every obstacle that comes your way with grace, persistence, and perspective. It is a must read for every woman who desires to live her life with purpose and authenticity." **~Raychel Chumley, Co-Founder of Big Blue Couch™ Coaching, LLC**

"Very real help. Very real hope. Very real heart. Friend, you are about to open the most creative and complete Toolbox on Overcoming I've had the pleasure to read. Mandy possesses the beautiful gift of making you feel like you're sitting across the table from her in a cute, cozy coffee shop, having her pour words of life into your cup and fill it to overflowing with her deep faith and contagious spirit.

Every word of this book is drenched in capital-T Truth...from the vulnerability of Mandy's personal sharing to the clarity of her study of Scripture to the conviction of her bold belief that each one of us is born to overcome. So, grab your favorite coffee and settle in for a life-changing ride." **~Laura Moss**

DEDICATION

This book is dedicated first to my mom. Mom – you overcame the devastation that no doubt came with the medical diagnosis that the doctors gave your daughter. You persisted. You met each challenge with courage. You put your trust in the Redeemer. Your example helped shape my reality. I love you so much!

This book is also dedicated to you, dear reader. I may not know your name, or your circumstances, but I know well the desire to overcome – a desire you have, or you would not be reading these pages. I pray that you find within this book the encouragement, grace, and boldness you need to rise up out of the ashes of your own circumstances!

CONTENTS

ACKNOWLEDGMENTS

Thank you Jesus for the gift of trials for without them, I wouldn't know the depth of your love for me. Thank you Jesus for the seasons of darkness for without them, I wouldn't cherish the seasons of light. Thank you Jesus for loving me enough to die for me and to refine me for without the refinement process, I wouldn't know myself. I pray this book glorifies you.

Nate – my handsome husband - thank you for encouraging me every. Single. Day. Your words of life have helped shape the woman I am today. I love you so very much.

Mom and Dad – thank you for loving me through the dark days and for teaching me to always walk by faith. I love you.

Raychel – without our lifelong sisterhood I honestly don't know if I would be alive today. Thank you. Thank you for grieving with me. Thank you for letting me fully feel my emotions. Thank you for speaking truth into and over my life. Thank you for helping me get back up. I love you tons. Always. Real.

Kristi Frahm – you helped shape me as a writer all those years ago in a high school English class and I am forever thankful for it. Thank you for being the first to read this book, and thank you for your friendship through the years.

Thank you to everyone who tried to knock me down and stop me. It only made me stronger.

FOREWORD

It was late Spring, and I was waiting on my mom's front porch for my best friend to call. Mandy was meeting with a publisher about her book that morning, and I could not wait to hear how it went. It would be a conversation that changed our lives and the trajectory of our one-year-old company.

The publisher loved the idea, and Mandy's writing style, but did not think the coaching heavy content would resonate with their audience. They wanted Mandy to make some major changes, revamp the entire outline, and resubmit the book. We had a big decision to make.

It seems like a no-brainer to just make the changes and get published by a publisher for the first time. It is every aspiring author's dream to get picked up by a major publishing company! However, this message was lived and breathed by both Mandy and I, and our clients. We were the original She Who Overcomes™.

It was sacred. And we were conflicted.

In the end we chose to keep the message intact and self-publish. We have not regretted that choice for one moment since. Helping a woman become a She Who Overcomes™ is our life's work. And it's my honor to write the foreword for this new edition. In our short amount of time together in these pages, I hope to share with you my season of suffering and the two choices I believe every woman needs to make when she finds herself in overwhelming circumstances.

~ A STEEL MAGNOLIA ~

"When it comes to pain and suffering, she's right up there with Elizabeth Taylor." ~Truvy Jones, *Steel Magnolias*

I have loved the movie *Steel Magnolias* for as long as I can remember. I can quote it word for word. I mean, what is not to love? The cast is star studded. The banter witty and quick. The portrayal of friendship and family amid grief and change is raw and relatable. It stands the test of time. It is pure movie magic!

And I am almost certain Truvy, played by Dolly Parton, was the inspiration for my short stint in beauty school. I wanted a salon just like hers!

A steel magnolia is a woman who is strong and feminine simultaneously. It is a concept that hails from the deep south and describes a woman who can be solid like steel, yet soft like a magnolia, no matter what life throws at her. She is equal parts tough and tender. To me, a Steel Magnolia is an overcomer. A She Who Overcomes™. This story of overcoming has been birthing in my heart since the first time I watched that movie.

There have been many times in my life where I have felt I could give Elizabeth Taylor a run for her money. One year after we published, *She Who Overcomes*, I found myself in one of the worst seasons of my life. Everything I knew went up in smoke when I chose to leave my 14-year marriage in the Fall of 2016.

After a nine-month separation, and failed attempts at reconciliation, I burned my life to the ground and crawled away from the ashes. I bore the wounds and scars of a woman who had spent nearly two decades loving a man who suffered from alcoholism. And I was broken. Mandy once said if you could have seen the invisible scars on my skin no one would have recognized me.

What I've discovered over the last few years, is your ability to overcome and rise up is directly related to your choices. Specifically, the choice to grieve and the choice to heal. Grief and healing are equal parts tough and tender. They require vulnerability and tenacity. But they are not the same. They cannot be skipped. And you will often find yourself walking both paths at the same time.

~ I CHOOSE TO HEAL ~

Honestly, the healing process was sometimes harder than the marriage ever was. It might surprise some of you to read that. But many women will understand the idea that healing is often worse than surviving. There are consequences you do not see coming. Embracing the healing process is for the brave only. The Overcomers.

I had to choose to heal (as much as possible) from my PTSD with therapy and EMDR. It was horrific and stressful to prep for these sessions. Who wants to dig up long buried, and sometimes fresh, pain? But the freedom I found from nightmares, intrusive thoughts, and the cycle of disconnecting was worth every hard moment. I fought for my healing and learned how to anticipate and handle triggers and what to do when anxiety flares.

Healing included me seeking out safe spaces where I could process my emotions and tell my story. I attended support groups where I could learn from, and link arms with, women who were overcoming the same obstacles. I fought for freedom and found truth again. I unlearned the toxic behaviors I had used to survive. And I discovered healthy coping mechanisms.

Choosing to heal helped me learn to advocate for myself. To trust my instincts and ask for second opinions. To lean into my faith and trust God, despite past abuse and gaslighting from Christian leaders. Healing from my past helped me break the cycles of sabotaging and people pleasing, to find wholeness again. It even helped me handle the yearlong battle with debilitating chronic pain and nerve damage that would hit its peak during the year of the plague…I mean the Covid-19 pandemic.

Choosing to walk through the healing process is hard. I won't lie to you. But girl…we can do hard things. WE MUST DO HARD THINGS! And I promise you that the woman who is waiting on the other side of your healing is worth fighting for.

~ I CHOOSE TO GRIEVE ~

Tragedy brings grief. It is a natural cycle that every woman must go through when something or someone dies in her life. Every season of suffering needs a healing season *and* a grieving season. You can try and avoid it but there are serious consequences and the grief never really goes away - it just compounds. You bury it alive. And I have watched enough scary movies to know that never ends well.

In the book, *On Death and Dying,* written by Elisabeth Kübler-Ross, we are told there are five cycles of grief. They each have distinct characteristics and clinical definitions. But a few years ago, I came up with a new way to describe the grief cycle when it comes to tragedy and loss outside of death. I hope this helps you along with all the other rich content you will find in this book:

Stage 1: Denial.

This is the numb stage. Where you pretend it does not matter, it did not happen, or it is OK that it did. You are fine. Fine. But everyone around you knows you are not. The good news is you do not have to do anything to move through this stage. Reality comes in due time. The bad news is reality brings anger. Lots and lots of anger.

Stage 2: Anger.

Oh, dear reader, I must tell you that anger covers deep sadness. But at this stage you are more *"I'm so pissed I can't see straight"* than sad. This stage is full of rage music, screaming, angry letters, and hot tears, and reckless choices. This is the stage "nice girls" try to avoid because we are taught anger is wrong, divisive, or manipulative. Hear me when I say anger is necessary and healthy. Do not stay stuck here with unexpressed anger. It will eat your soul apart.

Stage 3: Bargaining.

Oh, bargaining, you sneaky devil. I call this the "If only…" And the "What if…" stage. During this time, you will make bargains with God, and anyone really, to get the life back you once knew. Any bargain. For some people, this stage can come before the anger stage, right after denial wears off.

Stage 4: Depression.

This depression is the naturally occurring sadness that happens after loss. It is a dark level of sadness where you are no longer numb to the emotions and it's all too much. You are acutely aware that your denial and bargaining did not work and the life you pictured in your head will never be your reality. This is the crying-in-the-shower-hunched-over-holding-your-knees-listening-to-Adele phase. The "hold it together until the kids fall asleep" stage. I call it the "loss that settles in your soul" stage. But oh, sweet lady, hold tight. The sadness does not last forever. The light is coming.

Stage 5: Acceptance.

When you land here you understand that your reality *IS* your new reality. You no longer cycle through denial, anger, bargaining, or depression. It can be a mix of emotions because there is great relief in reaching this stage, but it can bring with it a certain sadness of its own. You start to rebuild from the ashes during this stage.

I know it sounds like a lot when you just read it. And I know it's overwhelming when you walk through it. But, dear Overcomer, choosing to grieve is worth it. Without it you will never fully heal from life's tragic moments and unforeseen obstacles.

~ TO THE FUTURE SHE WHO OVERCOMES™ ~

This book is a guide for every woman who wants to rise above the obstacles and crippling circumstances life throws at her. For the one who wants to lean into her faith and grow instead of letting life make her bitter and hard. And, for the woman who wants to stand up and fight for her dreams when tragedy sweeps through like wildfire.

Mandy is an Overcomer. A steel magnolia. A woman who has chosen to walk the paths of grief and healing with bravery, tenacity, grit, and grace. And in these pages, she beautifully marries her story of overcoming with the soul-stirring words of Revelation. *She Who Overcomes* provides a road map for any woman who finds herself wrestling with grief, pain, and doubt and not sure which step to take next.

In the chapters of this book, Mandy will inspire and equip you to overcome the hardship that come your way. She will teach you to rise up and fight for the one and only life you get to live. With everything you've got!

And I'm rooting for you too. I know the resilience inside you. You can survive. You can rise up. You can grieve and heal. You will rebuild beautiful things from the ashes. Yes, you might be battle scarred and weary when the dust settles. But you will also be tested and proven true. A warrior. A steel magnolia. A She Who Overcomes™.

With Grace & Grit,
-Raychel Perman
CEO of RAYMA Team, LLC and co-author of *She Cultivates Resilience*

INTRODUCTION
The Desire to Overcome

Tucked within the pages of the Book of Revelation are seven letters to seven different churches. I will be the first to admit that the Book of Revelation is filled with imagery and symbolism that lends itself well to confusion. However, a few years ago, my ears perked up as I read chapters two and three. In the NIV version, the phrase "to him who overcomes" is mentioned seven times. Seven times in just a few short chapters! The words sucked me in, danced upon my heart, and lit a fire in the depths of my soul.

I desire to be a "she who overcomes." An overcomer.

I desire to be the type of woman who rises above crippling circumstances and grows stronger after each obstacle. I desire to go through the hard lessons gracefully and let God chisel away the stone cold pieces of my heart that hold me back and keep me stuck. I desire to stay in the fight until the finish, never to give up, and never to give in to the schemes of the enemy that are meant to keep me from my destiny.

Life is more than endless days of work at a job that is

unfulfilling. It's more than daydreaming about the moment when you can sit on the couch in your sweatpants, feeding your face with cookie dough ice cream, while you live vicariously through the lives of your favorite television characters. Life is more than struggling through sickness and hardships, forever wishing things would be better.

It is about persisting.

Persisting during suffering. Persisting when you're weary. Persisting when the chaos of life threatens to choke you, cage you in, or hold you back.

Life is about finding the courage to resolve conflict with honor and grace, and being brave enough to live authentically while facing your fears. It is about letting go of past mistakes and weaknesses so the Redeemer can renew you.

Only then can life overflow with laughter, love, miracles, adventures, and meaning. That's the kind of life I want to live...the life of an overcomer.

I desire to be an overcomer.

Chances are you do too.

~ Mandy

1

She is Born to Overcome

In 1981 the medical outlook for a baby born with cystic fibrosis was not good. It was known as a child's disease because children rarely reached adulthood due to its life threatening severity and complications.

Sixty-five red roses symbolize this disease, a beautiful symbol for a treacherous disease known for suffocating its young victims to death. That was the reality of cystic fibrosis in 1981. The story goes that a child once had difficulty pronouncing "cystic fibrosis" so she would go around telling people that she had "sixty-five roses."

Mark and Mary Brakel were a young married couple preparing for the birth of their first child. One day, in the first trimester of her pregnancy, Mary found herself visiting a friend whose baby girl had recently been diagnosed with cystic fibrosis. She observed her friend giving her baby percussion, a therapy used to help loosen the mucus in the lungs. With cupped hands, the young mom was lightly pounding her baby's back, chest, and sides.

Thump, thump, thump. Thump, thump, thump. The rhythmic sound echoed through the room. As she watched this mom diligently perform the task of clearing out her daughter's lungs, Mary thought to herself, *"I don't think I could ever do that to my baby."*

Time passed and Mark and Mary welcomed their daughter into the world on December 4, 1981. She was born a few weeks early and weighed four pounds, nine ounces. When their daughter was four months old, Mary's mother, Agnes, kissed the baby's forehead and told Mary that it tasted salty. Agnes knew that a distant family member had been born with cystic fibrosis several years earlier and she reminded Mary that one of the symptoms was salty skin. Mary thanked her mother for the information but brushed it off saying, "Oh, I'm sure that's not it." Deep down she believed that bad stuff didn't happen to her family; it happened to other people.

Yet, there was no denying that something was terribly wrong with their little girl. At six months old, she weighed only ten pounds and had been diagnosed with a failure to thrive. She was sick with pneumonia or bronchitis often and spent more time in the hospital than a newborn baby should. On Memorial Day 1982, after a long six months of battling this unknown sickness that never seemed to go away, Mark and Mary ditched their plans to visit their family and finally met with a specialist who confirmed what they didn't want to hear. Their precious little girl had cystic fibrosis.

Denial, disbelief, and fear hit them like a ton of bricks the moment the doctor looked at them and said, "I hope you have good health insurance." They nodded their heads "yes", but they were in shock. Mark recalled hearing that the outlook for a baby with cystic fibrosis was not good; that it would be a miracle if she graduated high school. Their doctor reassured them that although that was a very real possibility, the advancements in medicine had come a long way and it was becoming more and more likely that their daughter could live to be eighteen, maybe even twenty years old.

Within a week, they were jolted into the unknown world of breathing treatments twice a day and having to learn how to mix the medication for each one. Doctor visits would now be a monthly requirement. So would pounding their daughter's chest so the mucus could be loosened up and she could cough it out. Suddenly the thing Mary once thought she could never do was becoming her new normal.

Even in the midst of fears and questions about the future, they determined to do their best for the sake of their daughter's health. They made sacrifices and vowed to give their only child the best life they could. They decided to give her a fighting chance. And…they prayed.

Through sinus surgeries and hospital stays, they never failed to remind their daughter that God was in control. They prayed for healing and sought Godly wisdom. They taught her to be responsible, but mostly, they taught her to walk by faith.

Decades later, Mary would recall a prayer that she remembered whispering when their lives forever changed on that long ago afternoon. It was a prayer that helped her stay focused on God through it all. It was simply this: "I won't ask 'why me, Lord?' I will simply ask 'why not us?' We will trust You to lead us through this."

Mark and Mary Brakel were, and continue to be, overcomers who walk by faith and believe in miracles. They are my parents, and I'm forever thankful for their sacrifices and examples.

I was born with cystic fibrosis. More importantly, I was born to overcome.

~ MARRIED AND BROKE ~

Obviously, I did go on to graduate high school. I even got married.

I remember the first time I saw my husband, Nate. We were at a college youth group meeting and I was singing a song as part of worship. I did not know his name, but I remember seeing this tall, handsome man with dark hair and a goatee sitting in the audience. He smiled at me and continued to worship.

A few weeks later, I was introduced to him at a prayer meeting. His heart for God was one of the most attractive things about him, even though I was completely oblivious that there was any attraction there at all. We became fast friends; best friends. He even vowed to help me get a date with a friend of his that I had a huge crush on. However, that particular date never happened because Nate and I spent all of our time together. After all, that's what best friends do. Several months later, we realized our best friend status had grown into a full-blown crush for each other. We began dating soon after.

From the moment I met him, I knew that Nate would be in my life forever, even though at the time I wasn't interested in him romantically. It just felt like home. He was trustworthy and made me laugh. He also wasn't scared off by, or afraid of, cystic fibrosis. That was important.

We got married on August 10, 2002 and our life together began. Seven years later we were confronted with financial hardships due to mistakes and stupid decisions. We were in debt up to our eyeballs and didn't even know it!

It happened slowly, with small decisions and seemingly harmless habits – a splurge on a business suit here, an overly priced car that we didn't need there. Often times I would get upset that my husband was working over sixty hours so I would find my happiness at the end of a shopping spree. Only it really wasn't happiness. It was more like a straight shot of adrenaline mixed with a side of guilt and shame. I had a shopping addiction and he just wanted me to be happy. We were both totally unaware what real happiness and joy was. So with each swipe of our credit cards we found ourselves drifting further apart from each other and deeper into the pit of debt.

When we finally figured it out, we were faced with either filing bankruptcy or selling everything we owned to pay our debts and begin a new lifestyle. Our pride kept us from looking at bankruptcy, so we pulled up our big kid underwear and began selling our possessions and scaling back on what consumed our lives.

Five years later, after paying off $160,000 of debt, we found ourselves debt free with a new financial outlook. There's obviously more to this story, but we will visit those details in later chapters. The point right now is that we recognized a huge obstacle in our lives and we did something about it. In doing so, we healed the problems in our marriage and grew closer. We overcame it! Why? Because...

We were born to overcome.

~ WHEN THE FLAMES DEVOUR EVERYTHING ~

One might think that overcoming cystic fibrosis on a daily basis while simultaneously getting out of debt is quite the feat. In fact, one might even think that our plate was full and there was no way that any more chaos could fit on it. However, I've learned that God's ways don't always fit into our perfectly planned agenda.

Chaos and pain never follow a rulebook. We were about to find out exactly how much of each we could handle.

The morning of October 11, 2010 was a beautiful morning. Streams of sunlight glistened through our windows and the air was still. It was one of those perfect weather days. I wasn't scheduled to work until noon so I spent all morning in prayer. This prayer time was different than the brief prayers I had in the past. This was bold and on fire. It brought about a peaceful sense of expectation in my heart that stirred me to the very core. As I paced the hallway of our three-bedroom apartment, Ajah B., our six-and-a-half-year-old Shih-Tzu, lounged on the back of her favorite plush, celadon green microfiber chair. She rested there, static, with only her big puppy eyes peeled on me, following my every move.

We had moved into this apartment only fifteen months earlier as part of our "We're Broke, This Means War!" game plan to pay off our debt and change our lifestyle. After looking at several pet-friendly apartments in our area, we decided on The Galleria. With spacious floor plans and an indoor pool, it was the Taj Mahal of pet-friendly apartments. Living in a pet-friendly community has its ups and downs. It wasn't uncommon to have a surprise turd left in the hallway by some four-legged friend who couldn't quite make it to the potty area. I'm not proud of this, but I once walked off the elevator after a long, hard day of work only to be greeted by a cute little puppy wandering down the hall alone. He decided that the best way to say hello was to jump on my legs and mark me as his personal territory, peeing all over my brand new shoes. Have you ever walked down a hallway with warm dog pee dripping around your feet and into your shoes? I'm sure I looked like *I* had just had an accident in my pants as I slowly waddled down the hall. Like I said – pet-friendly communities have their ups and downs.

Despite these sometimes-hazardous conditions, we loved The Galleria. Our home there was a three-bedroom, two-bathroom apartment with cathedral ceilings. The overly sized furniture we owned (of which had a price tag that was much too high for a couple in their twenties to pay for, but we were young and our priorities were a bit out of whack) fit the space well and it turned out to be quite a cozy atmosphere for hosting gatherings with close friends. Yes, The Galleria was a wonderful place to live.

As I prayed that morning, I thanked God for moving us there and for changing our hearts, freeing us from the bondage of materialism that had kept us blinded and unhappy for years. Several times the Holy Spirit prompted me to do things that were out of the ordinary for me. I walked into our bedroom, praying for my husband, and I saw his wedding ring sitting on his nightstand. I usually didn't make a habit of walking over to his nightstand, but that morning his ring caught my eye. My first thought was *that does not belong there!* Nate, my wonderful husband of eight years at the time, was a contractor so he rarely wore his wedding ring during the week in order to avoid possible injury. I was slightly irritated that he hadn't taken the time to put it in its correct place.

So I picked up his ring and walked over to my jewelry stand, opened the top mirror and placed his ring in the ring holder. Then I closed the top and continued praying.

I felt an urge to pull out my notes from a seminar I had attended several months earlier. The topic was praying with boldness. There were some key points that I wanted to be able to see every day, so I spent some time writing them out in bright markers on the marker board that was hanging on our wall in the hallway.

As I went through my notes, I thought to myself, *what better way to start practicing bold prayers than right now!* And that's exactly what I did. I prayed so boldly that I could feel a fire burning in my belly and stirring in the depths of my soul. What happened next was nothing short of a move of God. The words flew out of my mouth before I even knew what was happening. The last thing I prayed that morning was this:

"Lord, I don't care if you strip me of everything that I own! I will still praise you because what you did on the cross is enough!"

Talk about BOLD prayers!

Little did I know that by the end of the day, I would find out if I really meant that prayer.

•••

Right before I went to work that day, I got on my Facebook page and posted a status update. It simply said this: *Today is going to be a great day!*

It's funny to think about now because it actually was a great day. It was the night that was awful. It became the worst night of my life and forever changed the course of our path. It ruined me. It ruined me good.

Around four in the afternoon, I stopped back at home to let Ajah B. out. I was in a hurry because I needed to get back to work so I was busy multitasking, not really paying attention to her. She was dilly-dallying in the grass and taking her sweet time. I had to tug her leash several times saying, "Come on Ajah B. I don't have time for this!" Silly. We adults get so wrapped up in our own agenda that we simply forget about the things that matter in life. Poor Ajah B. just wanted to spend some time outside in the sunshine. She just wanted to stop and smell the roses! I was robbing her of that because I had to hurry up and get back to work.

When we finally got upstairs, I rushed into the kitchen to grab her a treat. She just stood there with her fluffy ears and big, brown eyes staring at me as if to say, *"Mom, don't you want to hug me? I miss you! What did I do wrong?"* I didn't even say goodbye to her like I normally do – I couldn't, I was in a hurry. Besides, she'd understand. (Now, maybe you aren't a pet person and if you're not, that's okay; but I have always been a dog person and Ajah B. is like my kid. We picked her out when she was just two weeks old and we've had her since she was seven weeks old. She is our kid; she is family.)

I shut the door and turned the key, with Ajah B. still staring at me with a sad look in her eyes. Only a few steps away from the door, something urged me to check on my curling iron. You know, in case of a fire. So, I walked back, opened up the door, and began to walk inside. I was immediately greeted by Ajah B., her tail wagging. Then I remembered that my hair was in a ponytail that day and I hadn't used a curling iron. Silly me, I was just being paranoid. I said goodbye to Ajah B., shut the door, turned the key, and walked away without petting her goodbye. Again.

At six o'clock, just two hours later, I received a phone call from my Grandpa. I usually don't answer personal calls when I'm at work, but this was just a little odd that he would be calling at this time of day when he knew that I was working, so I answered it. The conversation went something like this:

"Hello?"

"Yeah, Mandy? It's Grandpa. Did you know that your apartment is on fire?" He asked in a panicked tone. Grandma and Grandpa lived right across the street from us and made sure to let us know if they ever saw something fishy.

"What?" I replied, in a tone of disbelief.

"Where's Ajah?"

"She's. In. It." My thoughts began frantically screaming *this can't be real! It's probably just one apartment that is on fire. The firefighters will put it out shortly and everything will be fine.*

"Well, I will see if I can get a fireman to go up there. It's bad Mandy. I'll do what I can, but it's really bad," Grandpa said with sadness in his voice.

"Okay – I'm on my way," I replied. I hung up the phone and continued wrestling with the thoughts in my head. *I better call our resident manager to see what is going on. If it was really that bad I'm sure he would have called me by now.*

After briefly speaking with our resident manager, my fears were confirmed. It was true. Our building was on fire and the third floor was burning up with the ceiling caving in and flames coming out of the windows.

We lived on the third floor.

My whole body felt heavy. I don't remember everything that happened next. I know that I ran out of the building frantically without recognizing who I was running past. My chest was heavy and I felt like I had been punched in the stomach. It was hard to breathe, hard to see the road as I drove. I only lived about three miles away from work, and as soon as I stepped outside, I could see the thick, black smoke climbing through the sky. It was so high that people driving on interstate a few blocks away pulled over to watch and speculate with horror stricken faces. I tried calling Nate as I drove, but I just couldn't reach him.

By the time I reached the road to our apartment, I knew that Grandpa wasn't kidding. It was bad.

The Galleria was built like a hotel in the shape of a U. In fact, it looked more like a hotel than an apartment. Thick smoke billowed through the sky and giant orange flames jumped toward the clouds, tearing down our roof on their way up. Our third-story, cathedral-ceiling apartment was turning into nothing but ashes.

The whole time, all I could think was that my Ajah B. was in there and I couldn't rescue her. I tried to explain all of this to Nate when he called me back but the words that were in my head didn't come out right. He finally understood the mumbo jumbo phrases I tried to speak and headed home for an hour drive while I was left feeling like a horrible fur-baby parent. There was a thick knot in my throat and a very painful hole in my heart as I imagined my poor little puppy suffocating and then her little body being burned. It was beyond what I could bare.

Nate had advised me to get to my parents' house and stay there until he arrived. I'm not sure how, but I managed to reach their driveway without injuring myself or anyone else on the road. The entire ten-minute trip there was done in a bewildered stupor that I don't remember. My parents met me outside. They had seen the smoke so they knew something was up; they knew it was coming from near our apartment.

I sat on the concrete and stared at the smoke with tears streaming down my face. My mom picked me up and helped me into the living room, where I finally crumbled onto the floor with a huge wailing cry. Earlier that day I had read a quote at my chiropractor's office that said, "Don't cry because it's over, smile because it happened."

As the memory of those words danced upon my heart, I did the only thing I knew to do...I thanked God for Ajah B. and told Him how sad I was that she wouldn't see her seventh birthday, but that I was so happy that I got to be her mommy for six and a half years. And then everything went numb.

~ LETTING IT ALL SINK IN ~

Grief is heavy. Dark. Unpredictable.

There are no rules for grieving. As women, our emotions make us beautiful and complex. Yet, many times those emotions make it harder to bounce back when our world comes crumbling down. We grieve not only the loss of human life, but also the loss of what used to be. We grieve our dreams, our hopes, our comfort zones, and even the fur-babies that we are lucky enough to take care of and call family.

However, we must remember that grieving is a necessary part of the process of becoming an overcomer. Whether our lives went up in literal flames or in figurative ones, there will be a grieving process. We can't rush it. We have to let it run its course. We have to let every obstacle we face sink in to the depths of our hearts.

That's what overcomers do.

On the evening of October 11, 2010, my real journey of becoming an overcomer began. Cystic fibrosis, debt, and the apartment fire all snowballed into one giant pile of ashes that demanded to be dealt with. God was teaching me something through this season. He was teaching me that I was born to overcome...

And so were you.

•••

A few months later, after we had moved into a new apartment, I found myself flipping through the pages of my Bible. My fingers found their way to the Book of Revelation and I began to read. The words "to him who overcomes" jumped from the pages and grabbed my attention. In chapters two and three, this phrase is mentioned seven times. When God repeats something, it is worth paying attention to.

Over the next few years I found myself studying these verses; drinking them in. My soul was refreshed, renewed, and challenged by the instructions within these pages. I desperately wanted to know what it took to be an overcomer. The ashes in my own life were choking me at times, and the only comfort I could find to rise up and keep going came from these chapters. I wanted to be a "she who overcomes."

This book you are holding in your hands is about the story

that God has written in my life. It is also a chance to discover the story He is writing in your life. As we move forward through the process of becoming an overcomer, I will be peeling back the layers of my life as it began to unfold into this new territory of rising up out of the ashes. I promise to be vulnerable with you, but I'm also asking that you make me a promise – or better yet, a promise to yourself: that you will be vulnerable, too. With yourself. That you will courageously dig deep and ask God for guidance and wisdom as He helps you through this process.

Throughout our journey together, we will spend time renewing our minds by focusing on the truth. At the end of each chapter you will find "Truth About Me Statements." These statements are words of life that you can begin to speak over your own circumstances. I recommend speaking them out loud on a daily basis.

There will also be a chance for you to dig deeper in the "Personal Reflection Time" areas. Here you will find questions to journal through as you ask God for guidance and revelations. Additional Bible verses to study will also be included in several areas of this journey. Let's begin.

TRUTH ABOUT ME STATEMENTS:

- I was born to overcome every challenge that stands in my way. With God's help, I can become an overcomer!

PERSONAL REFLECTION TIME:

- As you read Mandy's story, what challenging circumstances came to your mind from your own life?
- How has God worked through these hard times?
- In what ways has God shown you that you are already an overcomer?
- What are some of the current "ashes" in your life that God wants to help you rise up out of?

~ section I ~

PERSISTENCE

2

She Endures Suffering

~how to persist when suffering~

~ JOURNAL ENTRY ~

October 12, 2010, 4:30 am

Brown. Any other day I would choose an orange, pink, green, or even blue pen. But today it's brown. It symbolizes the dust, what I'm made of. Brown.

Yesterday, God stripped me of every earthly belonging except what I brought with me to work. As I drove down the street toward my apartment building, I prayed that God would only save one thing for me – Ajah B. And as I saw the thick black smoke rising and the dark orange flames devouring the center of the building, I sensed that I would never see Ajah again. I experienced every emotion known to man tonight in the period of five hours.

Fear.

Panic.

Extreme hopelessness and despair.

Thankfulness that Nate was okay. Heartbreaking agony as I pondered Ajah's last moments. Thankfulness that God gave her to me for six-and-a-half years. Regret over how I neglected her at times and even shame over my selfishness at times. Grief. Laughter. Overwhelming gratitude toward the people reaching out to us, and a sense of peace as Nate and I thanked God for our safety and prayed for everyone else in our building.

And then...joy. Extreme joy.

At 12:15 am we received a phone call from someone at the Red Cross saying that Ajah had been found and she was okay. And she is okay. We are at the Staybridge Suites right now. Room 135. I'm emotionally exhausted and haven't been able to sleep. But I needed to get this all out.

This is the only journal I have now. And there's something freeing about that. My past is gone – all the memories, all the thoughts written down, gone. So now we rebuild.

We can replace the stuff. After all, it is just stuff. It doesn't define me. It's not who I am. My soul finds rest in Christ alone. I know that my God, Jehovah Jirah, will supply all my needs according to his riches in Christ Jesus. I know that nothing is too hard for God Almighty. We literally have nothing. We are homeless, though sheltered.

God, give me grace to walk this path. Your name will be glorified in all of this. Lord, give Nate grace, wisdom, and strength. Help me to uplift him. Thank you, Lord, for your miracles tonight.

•••

Life gets messy. In that messy pile of ashes, we hurt. It's painful. However, it is a Biblical truth that becoming an overcomer requires varying degrees of suffering. We would be silly to believe that we are exempt from it.

In Revelation 2:8-11, we are introduced to a church in Smyrna that knows a thing or two about suffering. Let's take a peek...

"To the angel of the church in Smyrna write: These are the words of him who is the First and the Last, who died and came to life again. I know your afflictions and your poverty—yet you are rich! I know about the slander of those who say they are Jews and are not, but are a synagogue of Satan. Do not be afraid of what you are about to suffer. I tell you, the devil will put some of you in prison to test you, and you will suffer persecution for ten days. Be faithful, even to the point of death, and I will give you life as your victor's crown.

Whoever has ears, let them hear what the Spirit says to the churches. The one who is victorious will not be hurt at all by the second death." ~Revelation 2:8-11, NIV

Reading these verses, it becomes undeniably apparent that there are varying degrees of suffering. Mentioned in this short passage are things like pain – both physical and emotional - poverty, struggle, fear of suffering, and fear of death. Read it again and see if you can identify these yourself.

Physical and emotional pain shows up in many ways in our lives today. The most common ways are through anxiety and panic attacks. Depression, anxiety, and panic attacks are twice as likely to happen to women as they are to men. Maybe you can relate to the feeling of your heart racing, your breaths shortening, and your mind drowning in fear as a panic attack takes over your body. I know I certainly can.

My first panic attack happened in the dark stairwell of our apartment. It was seven days after the fire and we were finally allowed to go back inside the remains of our home so we could see if anything could be salvaged. The ashes made the steps slippery, and we had to wear white paper masks over our mouths in order to protect our lungs from breathing in the harmful residue of the ashes. It made it harder for me to breathe and the darkness of the stairwell mirrored the shade of fear that was rising up in my heart. My mind reeled with questions like, *"What would we see at the top of the steps? How many ashes would be piled up, representing our lives? Would we even be able to recognize anything?"*

As I wrestled with these thoughts running wild in my mind, my whole body began to respond in fear and panic. I began to gasp for air. My heart felt like it was going to burst and the stairwell was spinning. Nate helped calm me down by talking to me in a soft, monotone voice reminding me to just breathe. I wiped away the tears that had spilled onto my cheeks and took deep breaths, focusing only on the next inhale and exhale.

~ SPROUTS WITHIN THE ASHES ~

When we first see the ashes, our minds travel through a frenzy of bad memories. We question how it got to this point. We feel insecure, threatened, and unsafe. Rarely do we stop to see the sprouts within the ashes – the richness that is growing because of them. It seems quite impossible to even find anything good because we are too busy learning how to endure the suffering of the moment.

What speaks to me the most from the passage in Revelation 2:8-11 about suffering is that even though there is struggle, there is also hope. Did you pick up on that, too? The Message version of this passage says, *"Don't quit, even if it costs you your life. Stay there believing. I have a Life-Crown sized and ready for you."*

As I stood there in the stairwell experiencing my first panic attack, I was faced with a choice. I could keep indulging in the thoughts that had manifested more fear, or I could choose to believe that God was doing something in the midst of all this pain. With each step forward, I began to remind myself that God was in control. After all, He had already provided a miracle by saving Ajah B. Maybe we would experience more miracles at the top of these stairs. Maybe there were some sprouts within the ashes and I just had to look for them.

We made it to the doorway of our apartment and as we crossed the threshold, we stopped in our tracks. Our mouths dropped. Debris was everywhere. Our eyes scanned the rooms before us as we tried to identify what we were looking at. Was that the kitchen? Or the dining room? Or was it both, now thrown together in a mess of unrecognizable lumber? It was hard to make sense of the utter chaos. Yet, right in the midst of the debris of ashes and wood, standing against a wall that was still in tact, stood the marker board I had written on the morning of the fire. We had several of these marker boards in our home, and this was the only one that withstood the flames. Not only that, but the bright words were still readable, and on that day, we were greeted with the following Bible verse written in fluorescent ink:

"And my God will meet all your needs according to his glorious riches in Christ Jesus." ~Philippians 4:19, NIV

The first sprout had been sighted. It was a beautiful reminder of how God was carrying us through this season of suffering.

God also provided another answer to prayer that day as we rummaged through the ruins. Nate's wedding ring was found without a scratch on it. It had been nestled safely in my jewelry case and we found it right before we left The Galleria for the final time.

All in all, God returned the two things we wanted most from this painful experience – our precious Ajah B. and Nate's wedding ring. The marker board with His promises on it was simply an added gift to help us through the tough times that were ahead.

•••

We all have seasons of suffering in our lives. Maybe there is one that comes to your mind right now. Maybe you are still in it and you can identify with some of the feelings I went through as you read my story. I do not know what is happening in your life today, dear friend, but I do know that going through the suffering and choosing to overcome it with God's help is better than hiding from it.

When we read Revelation 2:8-11, it can be intimidating. Especially when we read things like The Message version that reminds us to "stay there believing. Don't quit." The last thing we want to do during suffering is to stay there! It is hard enough to believe, but to not quit, even if it costs me my life?! These verses seem a little dangerous at first glance. Risky, even. Believe me, I get it. When I read them a few months after the fire, I didn't understand their full meaning. I was completely oblivious to the season of suffering I was still walking through. But I held tight to them anyway.

What I've come to realize is that overcomers embrace painful situations differently than most people. Overcomers willingly endure suffering because they recognize its purpose. They understand that skipping the season of suffering would be more detrimental to their lives than the suffering itself. Pain, poverty, struggle – all forms of suffering produce faith. They produce perseverance. If. We. Let. Them. That's the key. A true overcomer will go through the process of refinement no matter how uncomfortable.

My season of becoming an overcomer started the day our apartment went up in flames. A few years later, in May 2012, I stood in front of the mirror in my hospital room and was shocked at the face staring back at me. Hollow eyes, pale skin, sunken cheeks. Those were not the features I had learned to love; yet they were mine. They reminded me of how a friend of mine with cystic fibrosis looked right before he died a few years earlier. They looked like death. *I* looked like death. In that moment, I understood the words of John in Revelation: *"Be faithful, even to the point of death."*

During a season of trusting God and walking by faith, my body had experienced sickness because of cystic fibrosis. I will go deeper into the lessons I learned from this process in chapter eight, but, for now, I will tell you that God had given me a season of divine health for a period of two years. I was able to do things without medicine that I should not have been able to do, like run and have more energy. Even my doctors were astounded and confused by it. It was exciting and thrilling and I experienced God's healing power in ways I never had before. However, as that season was nearing its end, I was afraid.

Let me clarify – I was not afraid of dying, although others around me were scared for me. No, I was afraid of not following God's command. I was afraid of giving up because the path He had asked me to walk by faith was too hard. I was afraid of missing my calling because I wasn't strong enough to endure. But staring at my frail reflection, I realized that I had already been faithful even to the point of death. Nobody was threatening to physically kill me, but the disease in my body sure was trying its hardest to take me out. In that moment I made a choice: nothing could ever stop me from glorifying Jesus. I was going to trust Him and praise Him, even when things did not turn out the way I had planned. Shortly after I made that choice, my health was restored and that season of suffering was over. What resulted was a stronger faith, boldness, confidence, and a deeper desire to persevere no matter what! God's promises rang true in my life, and I'm better for it.

~ HOW TO PERSIST DURING SUFFERING ~

Stay there believing. Everything within us will tell us not to; yet, that is exactly what we must do. We must stay there and face it while believing that God is doing something in the midst of it. Let's take a look at this passage in Revelation one more time, only this time, let's read the full text from The Message version.

"Write this to Smyrna, to the Angel of the church. The Beginning and Ending, the First and Final One, the Once Dead and Then Come Alive, speaks:

I can see your pain and poverty—constant pain, dire poverty—but I also see your wealth. And I hear the lie in the claims of those who pretend to be good Jews, who in fact belong to Satan's crowd.

Fear nothing in the things you're about to suffer—but stay on guard! Fear nothing! The Devil is about to throw you in jail for a time of testing—ten days. It won't last forever.

Don't quit, even if it costs you your life. Stay there believing. I have a Life-Crown sized and ready for you.

Are your ears awake? Listen. Listen to the Wind Words, the Spirit blowing through the churches. Christ-conquerors are safe from Devil-death." ~Revelation 2:8-11, MSG

This version of Revelation shows us different forms of suffering. It also uncovers something else that is a little easier to understand than in the NIV version. If you look closely, it gives us two tools to help us overcome in the midst of suffering. It's a "How To" on persisting during suffering!

1. Be Brave

Notice that God does not say "fear nothing for you will not suffer." No. He says, "fear nothing in the things you are about to suffer." What He is really saying here is be brave. According to dictionary.com, the word "brave" means possessing or exhibiting courage or courageous endurance.

It takes bravery and endurance to wake up and face suffering every day. Moving forward out of the ashes of your circumstances in life is never easy. Many days we will feel like crawling back into bed and hiding beneath the covers. Many days we will want to drown our feelings in chocolate and lattes. Many days we will long for what used to be. If you happen to be walking through those days right now, know that you are not alone. These are all normal feelings. And I fully believe that God has a purpose for those days of mourning what was.

But sooner or later there comes a time to be brave.

Be brave when you are faced with memories of what used to be and your heart begins to crack under the pressure of it all.

Face it. Admit it. Remember what was, but also look for the lesson that was there. Thank God for those moments, and then, let it fuel you to keep going toward something better.

Be brave in the face of sickness and disease. Face it. Admit when it hurts but don't stay there dwelling on the pain. Put on your warrior face and do everything you can to get better while praising God in the midst of it.

Be brave in the face of financial uncertainty. Face it. Admit where you went wrong. Face the consequences and move forward on a new, better path. Let this situation be your stake in the ground to never again make the same mistakes.

Be brave. Be real. Believe that God has a purpose for this season of your life.

Overcomers face seasons of suffering knowing that it is healthy to mourn; they also know that it is imperative to courageously endure knowing that there will come a day when the sun will shine again. Bravery does not mean that we never feel pain; it means we get vulnerable with ourselves to both feel it and admit that it is there. Once we do that, we can begin to move forward.

2.   Walk By Faith

In this passage, we are also told to be faithful. In order to fully understand what it means to walk by faith, we must establish a solid foundation of what the word "faith" means. Faith can be defined as believing in something even when there is no proof. Many of us walk around professing that we are walking by faith, yet we cower in fear over our finances, our health, our marriage, etc. That is not faith. Faith can identify fear as a feeling and nothing else; it does not waver in the face of fear and it is not controlled by fear.

Hebrews 11:1 says that *"faith is being sure of what we hope for and confident of what we do not see."* Faith is a choice; just as speaking God's written words of life and truth is a choice. I've come to learn that the journey of walking by faith is an ebb and flow. Sometimes it comes easily, other times it is the hardest thing we will ever have to do. No matter what, faith is always rewarding.

But you must choose it…

When you are struggling with your health, and you are tempted to believe the lies that you will never get better…choose to walk by faith. Remind yourself that God promises to carry you, sustain you, and rescue you even to your old age and gray hair.

When you are drowning in debt and financial freedom seems about as real as a unicorn…choose to walk by faith. Seek out wise financial counsel and make the sacrifices needed to get on the right track. Put your faith in action by doing what you can *while* you pray!

When you are struck with depression and your world is unraveling in darkness and loneliness…choose to walk by faith. Believe that God is doing something through this season and that the sun will shine again. If necessary, seek out medical intervention for a season while you take steps to also improve your physical health with better nutrition and exercise. Resolve to rise up out of the darkness!

And when you are waiting for a dream to be fulfilled but it feels so far away…choose to walk by faith. Ask God for wisdom and guidance as you gain the skills needed for the dream to come to fruition.

Walking by faith does not mean that you pretend to not see all of the problems. It does not mean that you ignore the ashes. No. It means seeing them and choosing to believe that things will get better even when there is no proof. Believe that this, too, shall pass because God's word trumps all. His promises are always true, even if they don't manifest in the way that you think they will.

~ IT'S NOT ABOUT ME…IT'S ALWAYS ABOUT HIM ~

Ashes are rich potting soil for future beauty. In every season of suffering there is something to be learned. The day my feet touched the ashes of our old life, the only sprout I could see was the marker board reminding me of God's truth. As my eyes scanned over the remains of our busted and burned furniture, my heart put up a shield that protected me from the pain. It was all too much to take in.

The cathedral ceiling that once provided a beautiful backdrop for the morning sunshine was now gone. In its place was nothing but busted out framework and a gray sky. I walked over to the place where one of our armchairs once stood and realized that I was now standing on all of it. My fingers dug through the pile of ashes beneath my feet searching for a piece of fabric from my favorite blanket, a beautiful handmade patchwork of jeans and hand-painted pictures with my name on it. Grandma Agnes had made it for me out of her own jeans and gave it to me at my high school graduation. She had passed away the year before and I had hoped to cherish that blanket for years to come. I never found any remaining piece of it.

My heart still grieves over that blanket. Yet, even in those times of delayed grief that catch up with me from time to time, God is still teaching me something…that He is always here with me. He knows my hurt. He understands those moments when I just need to take a time out because the memories of what used to be are too heavy for my heart. He is always there to wipe away my tears and grieve with me. He doesn't like to allow pain to happen to His children. But He understands the purpose of the suffering. He sees the end of the story and knows that each chapter is important. Even the chapters filled with ashes and suffering.

Especially those chapters.

I have come to understand that enduring the suffering is never about us. It is about Him; it is about the lessons He wants to teach us so that His purpose can manifest in our lives. So we can become all that He has dreamed us to be.

Allow me to take a moment and play Life Coach with you. Could it be, my friend, that God is trying to teach you something as you endure this suffering? Is it possible that on the other side of this trial you will be stronger *because of* this suffering? Could it be that He has a precious gift for you in the midst of it all? (If you haven't figured out the answer yet, it is "yes!")

Sometimes that gift is there for you to share with others. But often that gift is just for you. A precious package with your name on it, hand delivered from the Creator of the universe. And on this package, that right now looks like garbage, is a love note. A love note just for you. And here's what it says…

Dear _____ *(write your name),*

I see your pain today, and I'm so sorry for your heartache. Even though it might not feel like it, I'm right beside you, carrying you through and sustaining you in the hard days. I didn't make you sick. I didn't force this disaster on you. It was never My intention for you to struggle when I formed you in your mother's womb. However, I did design you with a plan in mind…

I gave you a positive attitude to help you overcome the obstacles you would surely face during your time on earth.

I made you beautiful – the shape and color of your eyes, the color of your skin, your height and weight, your hair, your cheekbones, your toes, your voice; everything about you was designed beautifully in my image. And I love to look at you for you are marvelously and wonderfully made!

I gave you a smile that lights up a room and cheers others up. Oh, how My heart melts when I see your smile!

I gave you a desire to seek out truth and authenticity, so you could live freely.

I designed you with talents and abilities to share with the world around you. People NEED you! Don't belittle these precious talents and dreams I have placed within you. They are good enough in My sight!

I gave you a brain with the capacity to learn and apply new skills to help you make better choices and live a healthier, vibrant life.

I designed you with a faith that can move mountains. It is already in you, waiting to be activated!

All these things were knit into you from the beginning of time. When I formed you – and saw how beautiful your life would be – sickness and suffering were not a part of it. Pain was not a part of that picture. Because of sin, there are things in this world that you will never understand, yet all of these characteristics that I designed you with will help you overcome any circumstance that you face whether it is sickness, heartache, loss, or pain. I designed you to be an overcomer. You already have the traits you will need to help you along the way!

So look for the sprouts within the ashes. They are popping up left and right if you just take a moment to uncover them. Hidden within this suffering is a precious lesson that you would not learn any other way. Seek after Me through it all; hang on to Me with all your might. I am here and I will never leave you.

And one more thing…I am so very proud of you.

Love,

God

•••

Look for the sprouts in the ashes, my friend. I give you permission to type out the above letter with your name written on it so you can post it in your room. I also encourage you to take some time to journal through the following "Personal Reflection" questions, as well as speak the following "Truth About Me Statements" out loud.

You have been given the courage to endure this suffering. Don't quit. Stay there believing! Be brave, and walk by faith.

Oh yeah, and remember to look for the sprouts in the rich soil that these ashes provide.

TRUTH ABOUT ME STATEMENTS:

- I am brave because God says I am and makes it so.
- I am fearless!
- I am steadfast.
- I trust the Lord.
- I am secure in the Lord.
- I am able to walk by faith because God equips me and calls me to it.
- I will look for the sprouts that God has for me in every difficult circumstance.

PERSONAL REFLECTION TIME:

- Identify where you are in your journey by answering the following questions:
  o Are you in a season of suffering and holding on to your faith? If so, describe what that has been like.
  o Are you on the other side of suffering, walking as an overcomer who is already victorious? If so, write down the sprouts that came out of those ashes (a.k.a. the miracles that God did in the midst of the suffering).
- What has God taught you in your past seasons of suffering?
- Take a few moments to journal and ask God for wisdom in the current season that you are walking through. Ask Him to show you where you need to persist and endure.

RELATED WORDS OF LIFE TO STUDY:

One of the tips I've learned in my journey of becoming an overcomer is to speak words of life out loud, over my circumstances, and to post them throughout my home. On the following page are some related words of life to study when becoming an overcomer.

"We also rejoice in our sufferings, because we know that suffering produces perseverance; perseverance, character; and character, hope. And hope does not disappoint us, because God has poured out his love into our hearts by the Holy Spirit, whom he has given us." ~Romans 5:3-5, NIV

"Consider it a sheer gift, friends, when tests and challenges come at you from all sides. You know that under pressure, your faith-life is forced into the open and shows its true colors. So don't try to get out of anything prematurely. Let it do its work so you become mature and well-developed, not deficient in any way." ~James 1:2-4, MSG

"Now faith is being sure of what we hope for, and confident of what we do not see." ~Hebrews 11:1, NIV
"And without faith it is impossible to please God, because anyone who comes to him must believe that he exists and that he rewards those who earnestly seek him." ~Hebrews 11:6, NIV

3

She Never Quits, but She Might Need a Nap

~persisting when weary~

"All of our representatives are currently helping other callers. Thank you for waiting."

I wanted nothing more than to reach through the phone line and wring the neck of the digital voice speaking at me. After ninety minutes of being on hold, I just wanted an answer. A human voice. Someone to help me figure out how to fix the situation that had punched me in the gut when I got home.

My car keys kept luring me toward them, ready to flee the scene for cover at the nearest coffee shop. I was tempted to grab them, too, run out of the apartment, and never look back. I was desperate for a warm cup of liquid comfort. Anyone would understand given my puffy red eyes and quivering voice. Weary and completely overwhelmed, I stood in my bedroom staring at the doorway trying to figure out my next move.

Give up? No. Just take a time out and calm down.

Give in? Oh I was so close, honestly I was. I wanted nothing more than to give in to the temptation of fleeing the scene and drowning my sorrows in a latte; but that's when my eyes caught the opened Bible sitting on the shelf next to me. It's bright pink underlining grabbed me and drew me in.

"Give your entire attention to what God is doing right now, and don't get worked up about what may or may not happen tomorrow. God will help you deal with whatever hard things come up when the time comes." ~Matthew 6:34, *MSG*

Hmm. At that very moment I was very worked up about what may or may not happen. Ironically, just a few hours earlier I had enjoyed a health talk by a speaker who was sharing how to stress less and laugh more. Her witty visuals had the whole room roaring! Good thing too – those endorphins probably lessened the blow a bit. Even so, in that particular moment, I was worked up. My conversation with God picked back up, and I let out an overwhelming, crazy cry sigh asking God where he was in this situation that seemed so out of control. It really felt like he had abandoned me.

And then that verse showed up.

I had read this verse early that morning, shared it on social media even. In the dim light of the morning sunrise, it seemed like such a vibrant ray of hope. But here, with my very raw emotions, it felt like an anchor pulling me back down to common ground.

"Don't get worked up…"

It was a lifeline, coaxing me to give in to God instead of running to the liquid comfort that had been my go-to fix in times of turmoil.

With tears streaming down my face and snot clogging up my nose, I carried my Bible and notebook into the living room where God and I had a time-out together. In the moments that followed, He reminded me that He sees the scars on my heart and emotions. He's aware of every scab that is still too tender and raw; that bleeds again in moments of despair. He sees them and He's not scared off, mad, or indignant. He's there to help when the hard things come up. And while I can't say He gave me an answer to fix the situation right then, He was doing something important and necessary in the very depths of my heart at that moment.

You see, as soon as I turned my attention to God and what He was doing right then, I saw it. He was healing me. Always healing the deepest hurts, the rawest emotions, the fears that creep back in and threaten to choke me. He was healing me in the deepest way possible while giving me the strength to persist through my weariness.

He will do the same for you, too, dear friend.

During stressful situations, we have a choice. We can either give our attention completely to God or stew in our stress and make the situation worse. Women naturally have a tendency to do the latter because we are the more emotional creatures. We worry about tomorrow and let the fear of the unknown fester in our hearts. We want answers now instead of gracefully going through the process. This usually results in extreme fatigue and spiritual weariness. It is in this exhaustion that our fragile emotions run wild, causing the overcomer inside of us to be buried.

Think back to the last few times when you felt worked up, stressed out, and extremely fatigued. What did you do? Take a moment to write down exactly what happened, so you can see the proof right in front of you. We can't improve anything until we recognize first the pattern, and then the root of the problem. And often, the root of the problem is that we allow ourselves to get sucked into the emotional storm and force ourselves to forge ahead without giving the reigns to God so he can bestow us with the peace and rest that we so desperately need.

~ HOW TO PERSIST WHEN WEARY ~

As we journey through these pages together, there will be a total of three times where we take a detour from the text in Revelation to let the depth and richness of what we learn simmer. This is the first of those three instances. Let's take a moment and hone in on a refreshing verse in the book of Matthew. In just a moment you'll see that God has taken the time to give us some important advice on how to handle these emotional storms and the weariness that blows in after them.

"Come to me, all you who are weary and burdened, and I will give you rest." ~Matthew 11:28, NIV

Did you catch it? Read it again just for good measure. He says "Come to me...I will give you rest." Not, come to me and I'll send you somewhere else. Not, come to me and I'll nag you for not knowing better. No! He does none of those things. Instead, we find that we are invited to bring our weary, frazzled, raw emotions to God and exchange them for rest. Peaceful, restoring rest. That's what we really need when our fragile emotions run wild.

Yet, we don't do it.

There are many reasons why. Sometimes we feel guilty because we have laundry to do, meals to prepare, and a home to clean, so we brush aside our personal needs to rest and recharge because the pressures of every day life are caving in on us. Other times we carry crippling beliefs in our hearts that tell us we aren't worth it or that the world will fall apart if we take a break. (Both of these beliefs are rooted in pride.) And sometimes we are just plain old scared and afraid of following the strings of our raw emotions to find what's on the other end, so we ignore it. None of these reasons are good; in fact, they are all just a bunch of excuses. But we use them anyway. We push ourselves further away from God and wear ourselves down until there's nothing left.

This crazy cycle can no longer be prevalent in our lives if we want to be the type of gals who are known as overcomers who rise above the ashes of our circumstances! No, we must rise up and recognize the need to rest. It is the only way to persist when we are weary! We must condition our eyes to see that without rest, defeat is just a heartbeat away.

I won't beat around the bush though. It will be a bit challenging at first. In fact, you might not like it initially because it

42

will seem counterproductive. It will require you to be persistent in learning how to pause and assess your situations honestly.

~ THE DAY I LEARNED TO REST ~

The room was dimly lit as I sat at my desk staring at the computer screen, cell phone in hand. My weekly coaching call with my life and business coach had just ended, and I was speechless.

Scale back? Work fewer hours and get rid of some extra activities? How in the world was that supposed to help me?

There was a part of me that felt relieved. Someone had finally given me permission to say "no" to things that had been making me anxious and exhausted. They weren't bad things; volunteering at church as the women's event coordinator was really fun. But it took more time than I had planned. Building my business wasn't bad either, but it consumed my every waking thought and the pressure to succeed overwhelmed me. My "go, go, go!" habits were taking a toll on my health, too. I had just gotten out of the hospital a few months ago, and my coach lovingly pointed out to me that this path I was on would only lead me back there again…faster. Also, I couldn't remember the last time my husband and I had a real date. *"What is he even doing tonight?"* I wondered.

As I doodled on my notepad in the dark, I realized there was another emotion tugging at my heart. Fear. I was afraid that I would fail. Afraid I would let people down. Afraid I would never be enough, have enough, or do enough if I took the time to rest and scale back.

My coach asked me to trust her. Against all my natural feelings to run the other way and figure out a better solution on my own, I chose a new route that I had never willingly gone down before. I humbled myself to the authority and wisdom of my coach and followed her instruction.

Had I not obeyed that simple challenge several years ago, you would not be reading these words today. On that chilly January evening, she taught me a valuable lesson that strengthened me. She taught me the value of rest and when to say no.

We live in a fast-paced world. People can reach us faster and easier than ever before. Emails, Facebook, text messages, and tweets all pile up on top of our already busy lives. The kids need our attention, our husbands need our love and support, our friends want to find time for coffee. Somewhere in the middle of it all we lose sight of ourselves and who God designed us to be. This is when weariness sets in. This is when we leave ourselves open to those emotional storms that derail us and wear us down until there is nothing left.

Many "opportunities" that promise rewards of feeling great, helping others, and being successful show up, only to leave us feeling alone, exhausted, frazzled, and overwhelmed. Let me clarify something: it's okay to feel great. It's okay to help others. It's okay to be successful. But when we do it all at the expense of our mental health, physical health, our marriage, our kids, and our time with God, it's not okay.

We can never fully live the life God planned for us – the life of an overcomer – when we are stretched thin and hanging on by a thread of fragile emotions and wearied hearts. So we must be intentional and get back to the basics. We must build a strong foundation and then add in the rest from there. That means learning when to say no to something that doesn't fully line up with our priorities or goals. It means asking God for wisdom to know what to say yes to and what to walk away from. Some things will stay and others will need to be let go of for a season or even forever.

~ THE ART OF THE PAUSE ~

My personal experience with persisting when weary over the last few years is what inspired me to develop a technique called "The Art of the PAUSE" We use this in our offices at Big Blue Couch™ Coaching to help our coaching clients get into the habit of persisting when weary and making time for themselves while also getting replenished through God's restful peace.

You see it's not so much that we don't know how to rest and let God calm the storm within. Rather, it's that we don't have the mindset toward it. That's where the acronym "PAUSE" comes into play. Let's take a moment to uncover the meaning and application of this important skill:

P = Pay attention to your emotions.

From this point forward we can no longer ignore our emotions. God gave them to us for a reason! We must not be ruled by them, but we also must not ignore them. Instead, we must make it a point to pay attention to our emotions so we can accurately assess where we are at any given moment in our lives.

I don't know about you, but when I get overwhelmed, stressed out, and weary, it comes out in less than attractive mannerisms. Let's just be real, okay? I get whiny! Irritable. Snarky, even. It's a real treat to be around me when my emotions are out of whack, let me tell ya! The sad part about it is that my husband tends to be the one to notice it before I do. (Don't we love that, ladies? It's a double-edged sword when your man knows you that well, that's for sure.) I know I can't be the only woman on the planet who deals with this, and I'm praying that you're saying a big "Amen! Preach it, girl!" under your breath right now.

It is in those moments of raw emotions and hangry feelings that we must remember to pause and pay attention to our emotions. They are a big indicator of what's going on in our hearts, our minds, and our souls. When this happens, we must train ourselves to take it to God. Stop for a moment and say a prayer, or spend a little extra time in His word that day. We can't plow through our emotions and expect them to fix themselves. They won't. Burying them only makes the problem worse, and it causes us to be even more worn down.

When we pay attention to our emotions, it allows us to take the next step.

A = Allow time to rest.

I love the words written in Matthew that we read a moment ago. "Come to me, all you who are weary..." If Jesus can give us permission to rest, then it stands to reason that we can give ourselves permission to rest, too. The world is not going to fall apart if we take some time for ourselves to rest and recharge. But it's not a natural thing to do in this day and age, is it?

I'll admit that the idea of resting used to be a hard one for me. My personality can swing on the type A side of operating as a workaholic if I don't watch it. Several years ago, I would rest only when I was forced to because of a migraine headache or because my body had just shut down from pushing myself too hard. Usually that ended up with being forced to rest in the hospital for two weeks for what the cystic fibrosis world calls a "tune up." Not exactly my idea of a vacation! It took working with a life coach for me to understand that it was okay to allow myself to rest. In fact, it is more than okay – it is a necessity!

God designed our bodies to work six days and rest one. From the beginning of time, that is how the human body was designed. He even modeled this for us in Genesis by taking a day of rest for Himself after creating the world. Yet we push ourselves to try and be Super Women. And you know what? It's doing exactly the opposite; it's actually wearing us down and making us less effective.

Over the course of working with a coach for a few months, I learned the importance of scheduling a day of rest into my life every week. My husband and I devoted ourselves to practicing this skill of resting every week without letting household chores or other expectations derail us. I'm not going to lie; at first it was really tough. Perfectionism tried to rear its ugly head on more than one occasion as we developed this essential habit. I can honestly say that after five years of implementing a weekly day of rest, it is now an essential part of our lifestyle. On the rare occasions where life is really hectic and we have forgotten to schedule a day of rest in, we feel it. It shows up in our work, in our relationship, and in our energy levels. Allowing myself to rest has become an essential part of becoming an overcomer!

If we were sitting in my office right now, assessing your lifestyle in a coaching atmosphere, I would ask you to take out a pen and paper and write down your beliefs on the idea of resting. Oh, how I wish we could spend those moments together, you and me, face to face! There's something about accountability that opens the doors to overcoming the obstacles in our way that we weren't even aware of. So since we aren't sitting beside each other right now, I'm going to trust that you'll contemplate the following questions on your own:

- When was the last time you truly rested?
- How does taking an entire twenty-four hour period off, just to rest, make you feel?
- What excuses come to mind that make you feel like you can't rest?

Take a few moments to journal through these questions and get really clear on your own beliefs about allowing yourself to rest. It just might be the one tip from this chapter that changes your life for the better!

U = Utilize stolen moments.

Pausing takes creativity. In order to allow God to calm the storm within us, it is important to utilize stolen moments in creative ways. Resting is not the only way that our souls get restored. Filling ourselves up with inspirational Bible verses, audios, music, time with friends, and even engaging in our hobbies can also help us recharge. Get creative with how you fill yourself up! Here are a few ideas that can help:

- Use your time in the car to fill yourself up with an inspirational audio or your favorite music. Sing at the top of your lungs and have a dance party! Who cares if someone sees you? Utilize the stolen moments while driving to feed the part of you that loves music.
- Carve out thirty minutes in your schedule to make it to the gym or take a walk outside three to four times a week. If you're at the gym, use that time to listen to your favorite podcast, audio book, or encouraging music as you tune out the world around you and increase your endorphins. If you're outside, unplug from your phone for a while and just be present in God's beautiful landscaping. Breathe in the fresh air, pay attention to the sound of the birds chirping, and gaze upon the beauty of the open sky.
- Put inspirational quotes on your phone or pull up your Bible app while waiting in line at the grocery store or at doctor appointments to fill your mind with truth!
- Journal in a notebook or on your notes app on your phone about what your favorite hobbies are and then write down a goal of when you will begin them again.

Just the other day I shared these tips with a mom's group. One of the leaders asked me to share my favorite apps and podcasts since many of the women had never applied anything like this before. Here's a few of my favorite resources for you to go deeper with utilizing stolen moments:

- YouVersion Bible app – this app is amazing! You can get a verse of the day and read several different versions of the Bible on this app too. Best part – it's free!

- Calendar app – several years ago when I was retraining my brain to think thoughts of faith instead of doubt, I scheduled a message to pop up every day at 11:00 A.M. from my calendar app. The reminder would pop up on my phone, and it simply said the words, "If I had faith, I would say…" This helped me redirect my thoughts immediately and stole back some moments that would have otherwise been lost to doubt, lies, and despair. It's a great way to remind yourself and encourage yourself daily!
- Podcasts – my favorite podcasts to listen to are from Elevation Church, Coffee with Chris (Christine Caine, a phenomenal speaker!), the Catalyst podcast, and of course, the Girls on the Big Blue Couch™ podcast! (Yes, I listen to my own podcast episodes because they help keep me accountable.)

Challenge yourself to find creative ways to utilize the stolen moments in your life. You might just find that those moments turn into the most inspirational, revitalizing moments of your day!

S = *Say no.*

In her book, *The Best Yes,* author Lysa TerKeurst makes the point that "When you have a pattern of saying yes when you know you should say no, it's time to reevaluate some things."* Do you ever find yourself saying yes to something while on the inside your brain is screaming NO? If so, you're not alone. It happens to all of us from time to time.

Saying yes to too many things results in stretching ourselves thin. Then we end up placing guilt on ourselves because we feel the tension of too many responsibilities weighing heavily on our shoulders. Take some time this week to assess your priorities, your schedule, and your goals for this season of your life. Then find a few things that you could say no to, in an honorable way, so that you can make more time for the rest that your body needs. Ask God to show you how to say no to three things each week that are not aligned with your purpose.

It might feel a bit awkward at first to say no to things, but in the long run it will set you up for success as an overcomer!

---

*Lysa TerKeurst, *The Best Yes* (Thomas Nelson, 2014)

E = Embrace the truth that you are worth it.

At the root of our overwhelmed emotions and reasons for not resting is a belief that we are not worth it. That's really what it comes down to. But you know what? You are worth it! Jesus himself is telling you – asking you – to bring your weariness and your burdens to Him so that He can give you rest. He's not saying "Come to me when everything is perfect and you have figured out how to get everything done and be everything to everyone." Not at all! He understands how we have been designed. He knows there will be times where we feel overwhelmed, stressed out, and emotionally exhausted. And He is waiting there for us to simply come to Him.

You are worth it. Not because I say so, but because He says so.

Embrace that truth right now, in this very moment. Admit, out loud, that it is okay to pause, to take a nap, and to rest so you can be at your best for what God has designed for you!

~ REFRESH. RELAX. RECHARGE. ON PURPOSE. ~

I have a confession to make. When I sat down to write this chapter a few days ago, I had no clue what to write. My mind was blank and creatively tapped out. My heart flip flopped back and forth between believing I could do this and wanting to call the whole thing off and quit. What was the root of the problem, you might ask? I was exhausted! Physically. Spiritually. Emotionally.

Instead of pushing myself to forge ahead, I recognized the opportunity to obey the gentle nudging that God had placed on my heart to spend the day resting and drinking in His words of life. As I did, my mind was refreshed, and I could think more clearly. My anxious nerves and fickle doubts were relaxed and quieted. My soul and energy was recharged. That's what happens when we trust God's nudging; when we allow Him to calm the storm within.

Imagine your home is quiet right now. Your loved ones are enjoying a nap by your side. Maybe your dog is resting at your feet and you are all sharing a blanket on a sectional couch. Cozy, right? Peaceful. You're nestled in the corner of the couch enjoying a snack and maybe a warm cup of coffee as rain falls outside your window. Pitter...patter...the beautiful, soothing sound of rain.

It's not just a dream, dear friend. It can be your reality. Days like that are needed. They are vital to our souls and our bodies. Rest days shouldn't happen on rare occasions; they should be a weekly part of our schedule. Days written on the calendar with the sole purpose of doing nothing. It's biblical. It's healthy. It's a necessity for the life of an overcomer.

As we wind down our time together in this chapter, I encourage you to look at your schedule and carve out a day of rest. Understand that time won't ever open up for this – in fact, busyness and the always waiting To-Do List will beckon you never to rest – you must make time to rest. Be intentional about it for yourself and your family! Every area of your life will begin to improve when you do this.

Refresh. On purpose.

Relax. On purpose.

Recharge. On purpose.

Because she who overcomes never quits when she feels weary. She never gives up when she's tired. Instead, she recognizes that she needs a nap, takes a moment to pause, and lets God recharge her soul as she rests in His peace.

TRUTH ABOUT ME STATEMENTS:

- I believe that I am worthy of the rest God wants to give to me.
- When I am weary, I bring my burdens to God, and He gives me rest.
- I am able to schedule a day of rest once a week.
- I am dedicated to refreshing, relaxing, and recharging my mind, body, and soul so that I can be the overcomer God has designed me to be.
- I am capable of learning and applying the art of the PAUSE, knowing that when I do, God's voice will become loud and clear.

PERSONAL REFLECTION TIME:

- What habits and/or thoughts wear you out?
- When you feel emotionally and spiritually exhausted, what do you tend to do?
- What habits help you persist when you feel weary?
- What does letting God calm the storms within look like for you?

RELATED WORDS OF LIFE TO STUDY:

"For I have given rest to the weary and joy to the sorrowing." ~Jeremiah 31:25, NLT

"So we see that because of their unbelief they were not able to enter his rest." ~Hebrews 3:19, NLT

"There remains, then, a Sabbath rest for the people of God." ~Hebrews 4:9, NIV

4

She Tears Down Idols

~getting rid of the things that hold you back~

I'll never forget the day I saw him. His blue eyes made my adolescent heart skip a beat. My legs turned to mush, and suddenly all I could think about was the blond-haired boy whose face had just made my world stop. I didn't know his name. Or his age. Or anything about him really. All I knew was that I was in love...with a movie star.

This seemingly harmless crush quickly turned into a full-blown obsession as I researched who my heartthrob was. Every picture I could find of him was plastered on my wall. Every magazine article that was written, I devoured. Eventually, after two-hundred posters, I ran out of wall space and it was too much to just consume every article and keep stacks of magazines piled on my bedroom floor, so I did what any normal love struck gal would do: started a scrapbook. Three volumes to be exact. After homework, I would thumb through the pages of Volume One and memorize every feature and fact about this teenage boy.

Through my extensive research, I discovered that he was six years older than I. It seemed a bit old considering the fact that I was only eleven at the time. However, I knew that one day the age factor wouldn't matter. At Bible camp, as I showed my best friends the beautiful volumes of scrapbooks that I had designed, I would be sure to let them know that when I was twenty and he was twenty-six, the age wouldn't seem like such a big deal. I was convinced that some day, somehow, I would meet this boy, and we would fall deeply in love and get married.

I know, I know. You're probably thinking, "Mandy, girl, what did your parents think about this obsession?" That's what you're thinking, right? Here's the answer – they were thrilled!

Okay, yes, there were times where they had to reign me in a bit as my dramatic pre-teen emotions threw a temper tantrum because I'd have to miss a television episode of a show he was guest starring in. Or when one of his movies came out, and the closest movie theatre was over an hour away, forcing me to have to wait until their schedule opened up. They had to practice parental sternness in those moments for sure. But for the most part, they were thrilled with the idea of their daughter's obsession over an actor that she would likely never, ever meet. Why would this thrill them? Because as long as I was infatuated with this boy who lived worlds away from the small town we called home, I was oblivious to the real boys who had crushes on me. It seemed like the perfect answer to any worries they had about raising a teenage daughter – keep her attention on a boy she'll never meet, and she won't have time for the real boys down the street! Problem solved.

~ WHOEVER HAS EARS, LET THEM HEAR ~

Now, before you start thinking that I am condoning this type of obsession, we must return to the words of John in the book of Revelation. There's something important hidden within these verses that we cannot ignore.

"To the angel of the church in Pergamum write:

These are the words of him who has the sharp, double-edged sword. I know where you live—where Satan has his throne. Yet you remain true to my name. You did not renounce your faith in me, not even in the days of Antipas, my faithful witness, who was put to death in your city—where Satan lives.

Nevertheless, I have a few things against you: There are some among you who hold to the teaching of Balaam, who taught Balak to entice the Israelites to sin so that they ate food sacrificed to idols and committed sexual immorality. Likewise, you also have those who hold to the teaching of the Nicolaitans. Repent therefore! Otherwise, I will soon come to you and will fight against them with the sword of my mouth.

Whoever has ears, let them hear what the Spirit says to the churches. To the one who is victorious, I will give some of the hidden manna. I will also give that person a white stone with a new name written on it, known only to the one who receives it."
~Revelation 2:12-17, NIV

I'll be honest with you. When I first read these verses, I had a lot of questions. Like, who was Balaam, and what was his teaching? Who in the world were the Nicolaitans, and are they still around today in the twenty-first century? And what about this hidden manna and white stone with a new name on it? None of this made sense to me, and the questions swirled around in my head like a word tornado. Maybe you've got a word tornado swirling around in your head, too.

Let's unpack this verse by answering these questions first, so we can then return to the movie star obsession situation.

Who was Balaam, and what were his teachings?

The first time we ever meet Balaam is in Numbers 22-25. It's a crazy story that involves a talking donkey. For real! Yes, the Bible is filled with crazy things that actually happened, and talking animals are part of it. (Because of this, I'm still praying for Ajah B. to start talking to me someday. I would love to hear her story of how she survived our apartment fire! Just once. It has yet to happen...anyway, back to the point.) The story of Balaam isn't a happy story. You see he was a false prophet. Yes, he heard from God, but he also practiced the art of divination. According to dictionary.com, divination is "the practice of attempting to foretell future events or discover hidden knowledge by occult or supernatural means." Divination is dangerous, and Balaam dabbled in it. (Seriously, read the story!)

Balaam's teachings included not only divination, but also manipulation, idolatry, and seduction. We'll talk about these more in the next chapter, but for now all we need to recognize is that these habits do not produce overcomers. They just don't.

Who were the Nicolaitans?

The Nicolaitans were a group of people who conquered and controlled others for their purposes. If you search the internet for information on this group of people, you find that they kind of developed their own church of sorts. They worshipped idols and went against everything God set up. Are they still around today? Well, they maybe don't call themselves by that name necessarily, but there are people all over the world who practice this on a daily basis. It is a form of idolatry, and many Christians who love God and want to live for him have even fallen into the practice of idolatry...but we'll get to that part in a moment, too.

What is the hidden manna?

When Moses and the Israelites spent forty years in the desert, God gave them manna every day to feed them. Theologians believe that the hidden manna in these verses symbolizes the strength and endurance that God gives Christians to sustain them in their faith. This point is going to come in handy in the coming chapters.

What is the significance of the white stone with a new name on it?

In Biblical times, if people were accused of a crime, they would be sent to court, just like our system is set up in the United States today. Their case would be presented to a jury who would weigh in their opinions and then take a vote. Each voting member would be given two stones. The first stone, a white stone or pebble, signified a vote of innocence. The second stone, a black stone, represented a guilty verdict. The verse that talks about giving a white stone to the person who is victorious is significant because it represents Jesus telling the overcomers that they will be found innocent. His word trumps all! This verse is saying that we are set free through Jesus!

The new name is also symbolic because once we ask Jesus to be the Lord and Savior of our lives, we become a new creation in Christ. God has made each of us to be unique, and through Jesus, we can boldly walk with confidence in that design.

These are all important things to understand. Now that we have all of the confusion cleared up, let's unpack the part of this verse that focuses on the topic at hand.

When we read this passage in The Message version, we see the following words...

"Write this to Pergamum, to the Angel of the church. The One with the sharp-biting sword draws from the sheath of his mouth— out come the sword words:

I see where you live, right under the shadow of Satan's throne. But you continue boldly in my Name; you never once denied my Name, even when the pressure was worst, when they martyred Antipas, my witness who stayed faithful to me on Satan's turf.

But why do you indulge that Balaam crowd? Don't you remember that Balaam was an enemy agent, seducing Balak and sabotaging Israel's holy pilgrimage by throwing unholy parties?

And why do you put up with the Nicolaitans, who do the same thing?

Enough! Don't give in to them; I'll be with you soon. I'm fed up and about to cut them to pieces with my sword-sharp words.

Are your ears awake? Listen. Listen to the Wind Words, the Spirit blowing through the churches. I'll give the sacred manna to every conqueror; I'll also give a clear, smooth stone inscribed with your new name, your secret new name." ~Revelation 2:12-17, MSG

Read the whole passage from that version again and you'll find that overcomers stand up for specific things, like:

- Truth
- Righteousness
- Godliness

Though the word isn't used in this version, it is very clear that the main thing they are told to stand up against in this passage is…idolatry.

~HIDDEN IDOLS IN A MODERN WORLD ~

The idols of today look different than in ancient times. We don't make golden calves that we bow down to, but we often bow down to things like money, television shows, celebrities, our jobs, shopping, and even food. Think about it. Which of those items take up the most space in your thoughts and actions every day? How many times do you choose them over spending time with God? How many times do you choose obsessing about them over renewing your mind according to God's Word? I'm not pointing the finger here because I'm just as guilty, and maybe this is written more for myself than anyone else. I mean, come on, I was going to marry a movie star that I never even met all because I was being driven by an obsession! And that's just it – anything we're obsessed with becomes a form of idolatry in our lives that we must repent of if we're serious about becoming an overcomer.

Idolatry is serious stuff in God's eyes. Even if we stand up for truth and righteousness, and stand firm in our faith – if we have any idolatry in our lives it will hinder our ability to overcome the things in which God says we can. The book of Revelation is not the only place that this topic is mentioned. It's all over the Bible! For instance, we read the following in Exodus…

"You shall have no other gods before me." ~Exodus 20:3

This instruction sounds simple enough. Right? I mean we know that when we choose to live our lives for Christ, we obviously are saying no to other gods and other religions. When we believe God's Word is the Living Word, these things seem obvious. In the country that I live – the United States of America – we have the freedom to choose which god to serve. This means that I am not forced to pray three times a day facing the East (or is it the West?). I don't have golden statues in my home that I bow down to. In fact, it's easy to read this passage and think that it almost doesn't apply to me.

But then I walk into my living room and see the flatscreen television mounted to the wall. And I wonder…how many times have I let that flat box dictate my life? How many times did I get tricked by the illusion of living my life through the stories of actors on shows like *Grey's Anatomy, One Tree Hill*, or even my favorite short-lived show from the '90's' that my heartthrob starred in – *SeaQuest DSV*? Yes, in this country, with so many freedoms and luxuries at our fingertips, we can easily convince ourselves that we put God Almighty first and only worship him. But do we really?

"You shall have no other gods before me…"

We deceive ourselves by thinking we have this instruction mastered; yet we don't recognize it in the mirror. This subject of idolatry is one that I wish didn't exist. I don't recall whether or not idolatry existed in my life prior to my infatuation with that movie star. But here's what I do know. The day that I began to obsess over him was the day that I willingly opened the door when idolatry knocked on it. I invited it in and unpacked its bags. And as I did, it multiplied and spread to other areas of my life as well. Over time it held me back from God's best for my life.

"You shall have no other gods before me..."

Okay. Maybe you can't relate to my story of obsessing over a movie star, because that's just not your thing. I'll give you another glimpse of the idolatry that has existed in my past, with the hopes that it will help shed some light on any hidden idols in your own life.

~ THE SHOPPING BAN OF 2008 ~

Remember in Chapter One how I explained that my husband and I went through a season of extreme debt? Well, a few years prior to our apartment fire, I realized how dysfunctional my shopping addiction was. It is not normal to go to a store, see a pair of shoes, and then fall asleep dreaming about said pair of shoes! Not normal at all! That is dysfunctional on so many levels! But I confess that this happened to me on more than one occasion. In fact, I still remember to this day dreaming about a beautiful pair of crimson red boots that I wanted so badly. I dreamt about them for months! Nate ended up getting them for me for Christmas, and, oh, how I loved those shoes!

There were other times where my love for shopping and shoes drove me to make bad decisions that resulted in buying a pair of pointy toe stilettos that were a size too small just because I loved them. After wearing them for four hours at work one day, I remember going home for lunch and having to ice my feet just so I could get my swollen toes back into the shoes! Crazy. I admit it.

Even though I was unaware of what I was really dealing with at the time, I knew it was serious enough that it had to be addressed because our finances and my sanity were being affected. So I put myself on something I called "the shopping ban of 2008." It was a fascinating experience that my friends even recall to this day. I wrote the following in my journal about the lessons that God taught me just within a few short months of applying this important ban on shopping:

~ JOURNAL ENTRY ~

<u>July 7, 2008</u>

In January of this year I made a vow to stop doing the one thing that brought me instant gratification (not to mention instant debt) - SHOPPING!

I decided that this would be the year I cure the shopping addiction that had been growing over the last several years. You know, the addiction where you actually dream of that pair of red stiletto heals until finally they live in your well-stocked closet, yet you don't wear them for fear of ruining them in the rain or the mud. Or that constant need to buy every single shade of gray suit you see at your favorite store because it will look amazing on you, even though you already have three gray suits that are now collecting dust because you don't have enough reasons to wear them.

Yep, I had a problem, and since recognizing that problem is the first step in recovery, I figured the second step would be to stop cold turkey! So, I have been adhering to the following guidelines for seven months now:

1. Unless it is a necessity, I don't need to buy it. (Clothes, shoes, earrings, necklaces, etc. - however makeup does not count because that, in my world, is a necessity, and has never been my addiction.)

2. The only exception to this shopping ban is if someone gives me money and puts stipulations on it such as when it can be used and what for.

That being said, this past Saturday, after several months of steering clear of the mall and any sales that would tempt me, I went shopping. I was given some money from my grandma last week and was told that I can't save it, but instead I need to buy myself some clothes. (Not sure if she was trying to tell me something about my wardrobe, but I wasn't about to waste this opportunity.)

So there I was in the mall, cash in hand, and ready for the hunt. There was just one problem - I wasn't finding a lot of prey out there to add to my collection. You see, since I've stopped shopping, I've stopped dreaming about things that I don't need. I've stopped obsessing over every cute outfit in a catalog, and I've found that I am beginning to be more picky about what ends up in my wardrobe. I have come to care more about what I spend my money on.

I have to say, this shopping ban is something I wasn't sure I could pull off. But I'm finding that the changes in my attitude, and more importantly the changes in my heart, are well worth the sacrifice of having the perfect outfit. God is teaching me so much during this time of no shopping, that I don't even have the desire to shop. I just don't think about it anymore. And you know what? It's very liberating!

•••

At the time I did not recognize this bad habit for what it was – idolatry. I just thought it was another addiction, much like my movie star obsession, that needed to be addressed. Hear me when I say this – any addiction is a form of idolatry because it takes your eyes off of God and traps you into a lifestyle of being controlled by the very thing that you are addicted to or obsessed with. That is the essence of idolatry!

~ GETTING RID OF THE THINGS THAT HOLD US BACK ~

According to dictionary.com, idolatry has two definitions. The first is obviously, the worship of idols (any person or thing regarded with blind admiration, adoration, or devotion). The second is "excessive or blind adoration, reverence, devotion, etc." We must not only understand what idolatry is, but also recognize the dangers of idolatry and be intentional about getting rid of it. If we don't, it will hold us captive; it will hold us back from everything God has for us.

Getting rid of idolatry is a continual process. We must reassess on a regular basis where the focus of our hearts is. Ask God to show you the things that are holding you back. What are you holding onto so tightly that it clouds your vision to what God has for you? These are the questions we must be persistent in asking.

In the weeks following our apartment fire, I marveled at how liberating it was to not be held captive by my possessions. Losing everything you own and starting over with just the basics teaches you an important lesson in what it means to be ruled by "things." Often when people would ask how we were doing, they would end their sentence with the words, "I just can't imagine what it would be like to lose all my stuff."

Kind of sad, isn't it? I will admit that, yes, there are some sentimental items that I will always miss because the memories attached to them are ones that I hold dear to my heart. But when it really comes down to it, my life is so much better now that I know what it's like to be set free from the bondage of material things. I'm actually thankful for the fact that we didn't have apartment insurance because if we had, the responsibility of trying to remember every item for documentation would have been overwhelming. Instead of combing through my memories of our stuff in the weeks after the fire, I was able to spend time with God, allowing Him to rebuild my foundation on Heavenly things rather than material things.

Idols only slow us down and reroute our focus to things that do not matter. God has so much more for us! Girlfriend, God is calling us to be overcomers who tear down the idols so that we can be free to move forward in the life he has planned for us. He is asking us to stand firm in our faith and stand up for what is right, even when it doesn't look like what everyone else is doing. Sometimes that means turning the television off and listening to a podcast or reading our Bible instead. Other times it means avoiding the mall so we don't get sucked into buying another pair of shoes that we really don't need. Most often it means reassessing our habits on a daily basis to make sure that nothing hinders us from God's best for our lives.

Recently I noticed this ugly thing called idolatry show up in my life again. It was a little tricky to identify, yet there it was, plain as day and right under my nose, or rather, my thumbs. My Facebook app had become a form of idolatry for me. It wasn't so much Facebook on my iPad or computer. For some reason I could implement healthy boundaries with those devices. However, on my phone, I found myself mindlessly scrolling through my newsfeed the moment I woke up and hundreds of times throughout the day. I would sense God telling me, "Mandy, spend some time with me, in my Word before you start your day." My response would be, "In a minute, God." Before I knew it, thirty minutes had passed, and I was still scrolling away mindlessly.

It was beyond distracting! Not only that, it fed fear and chaos into my mind as I read news stories of all of the horrible things happening in the world. It also made me late and behind schedule almost every day. I felt frazzled, and precious time with God was constantly stolen from me because of it.

Healthy boundaries need to be put in place to protect our minds, bodies, and souls from the treacherous aftermath of idolatry. One of the ways that I erased the idolatry of social media was by deleting the apps that were the problem from my phone. I also put my Bible app in a prominent place on my phone so that I could see it right away in the morning. It felt a bit strange at first to feel my fingers sliding through my screen in search of the Facebook app, but eventually it got easier, and the chains of bondage fell off within hours of making the decision to let it go!

When it comes down to it, overcomers don't give in. They don't ride the fence. Instead, they stand firm when others crumble.

They stand up for what they believe when others crack. God warns us to stand firm in our faith and boldly stand up against idolatry. In order to do this, we must learn to set boundaries so that we can serve God whole-heartedly. We've got to be willing to understand our obsessive tendencies enough to admit them, repent of them, and then be intentional about not going back down that path. That's how an overcomer persists in getting rid of the things that hold her back. And when she does this...

God gives her strength and endurance to keep overcoming when new idols threaten to hold her back.

God sets her free and gives her the verdict of "Innocent!"

She will begin to notice things like manipulation and idolatry faster than before, and then she'll quickly redirect her course according to God's will.

That's what happens when you choose to become a "she who overcomes" by tearing down the idols.

Maybe you have struggled with similar obsessions and addictions in your own life. Or maybe the idolatry that has been hiding in plain view is something entirely different. No matter what it has been, today can be a new start. Let this moment, right now, be the moment where you rise up and take a stand against the idolatry that has taken your eyes off of God's best for you. Let this moment be your fresh start to tear down the idols and rise out of the ashes as an overcomer.

•••

Dear Jesus,

Forgive me for the idols that I have allowed in my life. I believe that you have made me free from all sin and guilt, and that you call me pure and spotless. Jesus, I ask that you'll purify my life right now. Cleanse me and give me a stronger boldness for your truth. Supply me with the "hidden manna" – the strength to stand firm in my faith as I become an Overcomer in Christ.

In Jesus' name, Amen

TRUTH ABOUT ME STATEMENTS:

- I stand firm in my faith.
- I am able to rise above idolatry and not give in to it from this point forward!
- I am made new in Christ; therefore, my past addictions can be overcome.
- I will not deny Christ, but I will stand up for truth and righteousness.

PERSONAL REFLECTION TIME:

- How has idolatry showed up in your past?
- What forms of idolatry exist in your life right now?
- In what ways is God asking you to take a stronger stand for truth, righteousness, and Godliness?

RELATED WORDS OF LIFE TO STUDY:

"Blessed is the one who does not walk in step with the wicked or stand in the way that sinners take or sit in the company of mockers, but whose delight is in the law of the Lord, and who meditates on his law day and night." ~Psalm 1:1-2

"Some trust in chariots and some in horses, but we trust in the name of the Lord our God. They are brought to their knees and fall, but we rise up and stand firm." ~Psalm 20:7-8

"But we do not belong to those who shrink back and are destroyed, but to those who have faith and are saved." ~Hebrews 10:39

"So do not throw away your confidence; it will be richly rewarded. You need to persevere so that when you have done the will of God, you will receive what he has promised." ~Hebrews 10:35

"I urge you, brothers and sisters, to watch out for those who cause divisions and put obstacles in your way that are contrary to the teaching you have learned. Keep away from them. For such people are not serving our Lord Christ, but their own appetites. By smooth talk and flattery they deceive the minds of naive people." ~Romans 16:17-18

"My son, pay attention to what I say; turn your ear to my words. Do not let them out of your sight, keep them within your heart; for they are life to those who find them and health to one's whole body. Above all else, guard your heart, for everything you do flows from it." ~Proverbs 4:20-23

"Therefore, if anyone is in Christ, the new creation has come: The old has gone, the new is here!" ~1 Corinthians 5:17

"So if the Son sets you free, you will be free indeed." ~John 8:36

~ section II ~

COURAGE

5

She Deals with the Jezzies

~courage to resolve conflict~

Boisterous laugher spilled over the dinner table as my two best friends and I enjoyed a much needed girls' night out. The beautiful women sitting across from me had become more than just best friends. We were sisters in the deepest way possible, without sharing any DNA. Through extreme hardships and exciting victories, Raychel and Madison had become the gals that I turned to when I needed someone to talk to other than my husband. They were, and still are, my people. And on this frigid January evening, we all drew strength and encouragement from the support that only best girlfriends can give. Laughter really is the best medicine.

Even among the best of friends, silly habits can be hard to break. For reasons unbeknownst to me, I found myself going through the motions of scrolling through my phone to check if there were any urgent messages on social media or email. Even now, almost a year later, I'm still trying to decide whether or not this was a wise decision. My email showed that I had a somewhat

71

urgent message regarding an upcoming class I was to teach, so I decided to open it and quickly skimmed the content.

Every hair on my body stood up as I read the words nestled within the electronic letter. The fun girls' night out came to a jolting stop in an instant with just the swipe of a finger on my phone, and my friends could read it all over my face. Rejection. Hurtful words. Manipulation. Blaming. They all screamed at me through the pixelated letters and threatened to choke me out. Confusion ran rampant as I tried to figure out what I had done wrong. I passed the phone to my friends and then excused myself to the bathroom while I tried to regain my composure. Instead of finding the confidence I had hoped to gain in those few moments alone, I was met with a panic attack that left me feeling unworthy, incompetent, and not good enough.

This, my friend, was the first night I recognized a full-on personal attack of the Jezebel Spirit.

~ TOLERATING REVENGE AND JEALOUSY ~

At first glance, words like revenge, manipulation, and jealousy can seem like clever marketing for the next blockbuster movie. In reality, these are just a sliver of the characteristics and behaviors that we as women wrestle with from time to time. They do not form strength; they crush it. They do not create winners; they destroy them. These qualities are the exact opposite of what overcomers should embrace.

In Revelation 2:18-29 we see a letter to the church in Thyatira that seems uplifting at first, but then quickly takes a turn that addresses this very issue. Let's read it together...

"These are the words of the Son of God, whose eyes are like blazing fire and whose feet are like burnished bronze. I know your deeds, your love and faith, your service and perseverance, and that you are now doing more than you did at first. Nevertheless, I have this against you: You tolerate that woman Jezebel, who calls

herself a prophetess. By her teaching she misleads my servants into sexual immorality and the eating of food sacrificed to idols. I have given her time to repent of her immorality, but she is unwilling. So I will cast her on a bed of suffering, and I will make those who commit adultery with her suffer intensely, unless they repent of her ways. I will strike her children dead. Then all the churches will know that I am he who searches hearts and minds, and I will repay each of you according to your deeds. Now I say to the rest of you in Thyatira, to you who do not hold to her teaching and have not learned Satan's so-called deep secrets (I will not impose any other burden on you): Only hold on to what you have until I come.

To him who overcomes and does my will to the end, I will give authority over the nations—

'He will rule them with an iron scepter; he will dash them to pieces like pottery' – just as I have received authority from my Father. I will also give him the morning star. He who has an ear, let him hear what the Spirit says to the churches." ~Revelation 2:18-29

Before we dive into the rich content of this passage, let's celebrate what these people were doing right. First, they were displaying God's love. They had faith. They persevered, they served others, and they did all of this while building their skill. These are all good things! But then they took a turn and made a big mistake that had the potential to cost them dearly. And here's why we must pay attention, because even when we are doing many things right, we can risk making big mistakes if we do not remain teachable and stand firm in our convictions. The mistake that had the potential to derail everything was this: they "tolerated" Jezebel.

In order to understand fully why this was such a problem, we need to journey through a quick history lesson. In 1 Kings 16:29-34, 1 Kings 18 and 19, and 2 Kings 9:30-37 we get a glimpse of who Jezebel was. She wasn't someone to strive to be like, let alone tolerate. She was evil, and she had influence that brought about destruction to nations. She was the Queen of Israel long after Kings David and Solomon. She killed the Lord's prophets, and she urged her husband to sell himself to evil and wicked actions. The Bible describes them as follows:

"There was never a man like Ahab, who sold himself to do evil in the eyes of the Lord, urged on by Jezebel his wife. He behaved in the vilest manner by going after idols,..."
~1 Kings 21:25-26, NIV

The difference between these two rulers – Ahab and Jezebel – is that Ahab eventually humbled himself before God. (1 Kings 21:27-29) Jezebel never did, and because of this, she died a horrible death of being eaten by wild dogs. Ick!

The Jezebel spirit is a wicked spirit that still exists to this day, and in order to live life fully as an overcomer, we must not tolerate it or operate in it. Okay, so you might be wondering a few things, like what exactly is the Jezebel spirit, and why is tolerating it so bad? Well, just because she died a horrible death in ancient times doesn't mean that the things she stood for have vanished. Not at all. Some of the bad habits and attitudes that Jezebel stood for include:

- Control
- Manipulation
- Revenge
- Jealousy
- Twisting the words of God and others
- Rebellion
- Guilt (guilting others)
- Blame (blaming others)
- Selfishness
- Arrogance
- Pride

- Idolatry
- Condescending attitude
- Seduction
- Confusion
- Dissension
- Lying
- Distrust

These are just a handful of her nasty habits and thought patters (let's call them the Jezzies), and none of them produce an Overcomer. Not. A. Single. One. That's why we can't tolerate the Jezebel spirit. Because once we start, it wraps around every facet of our lives until the lines become so blurred that we no longer see a right or a wrong. We see indifference. We see gray. God doesn't stand for that. He stands for truth. Always.

~ RECOGNIZING YOUR PERSONAL JEZZIE TENDENCIES ~

Though I'm not proud of it, there have been times in my life where a spirit of Jezebel started to influence me. In fact, I can trace it as far back as high school. At the beginning of my junior year of high school, when my first boyfriend broke up with me, I wanted nothing but revenge. And it tasted sweet when I got it! At first. It came up served on a platter of eventually going out with him again, only this time, I cut the ties and broke his heart. Wiped my hands clean. Made the scores even. An eye for an eye. (Or in this case, a broken heart for a broken heart.)

There have been countless other experiences in my life that involved jealousy, control, guilt, blame, selfishness (lots of that), pride, idolatry, and even seduction. Honestly, the list goes on and on, and the stories are intertwined sometimes with more than one nasty quality. It took going through a season of humbling and repentance to get rid of this ugly spirit. It still tries to creep in sometimes, but I've made the decision to no longer tolerate it. So when I recognize it's filthy little fingers wrapped around the doorknob of my heart, I repent and pray it away…fast!

You see, as hard as it is most times, Overcomers get real with themselves and with God. They embrace vulnerability so that the biggest Overcomer of all time – Jesus Christ – can expose the weaknesses, wash them clean, and replace them with His strengths! Overcomers know this. They desire this. They won't quit until they experience this.

~ WHEN CHURCH FEELS LIKE HIGH SCHOOL ~

With every fiber in my being, I wish someone else would shed light on this topic. I've hemmed and hawed about this subject matter, often crying out to God, "Please send someone else!" But for some reason, God has called me to rise up and speak out about the Jezzies that have infiltrated our relationships, families, workforces, and sadly, even our churches. He doesn't always give me warm fuzzy messages, if you know what I mean!

The story that I shared at the beginning of this chapter happened within the four walls of a church. That's right, I said it. The women that were in leadership in a church that I had grown to love were operating in this spirit, and it was tearing friendships, families, and the church body apart. It was attacking people on personal levels as well and creating doubt, unbelief, and more pain than should ever happen from the family of God. But this isn't an isolated instance; it's happening in many churches, and it's time that we stand up against this spirit.

The church was never meant to be a place that hurts people. God's plan was…IS…for the church to be a safe place for the lost, the broken, and all the misfits who didn't seem to make it on Santa's sleigh. Wait. That seems a bit misplaced, especially since as I type this we are heading into summer. Or does it?

That's how the church should be in God's eyes. A place for the broken. A safe place for wounded hearts. Not always in a building, but in a group of people who are willing to celebrate everyone's strengths while simultaneously accepting and helping overcome their weaknesses. Yet in many churches across America, it has become the opposite: an elite sorority club that pats you on the back with a smile, then a high five yelling "You ROCK, Sister Friend!" only to turn around and list all of your flaws and call you bad names all in the name of leadership and wisdom. (By the way, that's called gossip, not leadership.)

Think this is exaggerating? Think again.

It's happening. It has happened to me, to people I love dearly, and to other people I know. And it has to stop. (Since I'm being honest, I will admit that I have done it to others without meaning to as well. After all, I did just admit to my own Jezzie tendencies on the preceding pages.)

Women seem to get the brunt of it. We do it to ourselves out of insecurity and feigned confidence. Men do it, too, although not as often and not as mean. With every snarling word and fake smile, hearts get wounded, and the church gets buried deeper and deeper into the pit of high school, and no body – absolutely no body – wants to go back to high school. There's got to be more. Jesus died for MORE. Than. This.

"But what can be done?" you might ask. Well, in order to overcome this high school church group mentality trend, we must be willing to rise up and do the one thing that might seem counterproductive at first sight. We must face it head on. God is serious about getting rid of this spirit, and that's what we're dealing with when we peel back the layers of a church that feels like high school.

It's easy to point fingers and say that someone else has a Jezebel spirit. We blame and ask others to "pray for that girl to be set free," and while this seems like a noble thing to do, this sort of action does nothing except play into the Jezzies even deeper. You see, the things that bother you and bug you to no end about someone else are usually just a mirror of what you won't change or admit to in your own life. (Ouch! I know, trust me friend, it's painful for me, too! No warm fuzzies here.)

So here's the part where we rise up and do something about it. Ready? While it probably feels like everyone is against you at times and that you're the misfit toy staring up in the sky at all the lucky toys on Santa's sleigh, I assure you, you're not alone in this. I'm right there with you.

~ THE HONOR CODE OF CONFLICT RESOLUTION ~

We will never overcome the Jezzies by operating in them, no matter where they show up. That will only result in making the problems worse and the friendship, relationship, or overall environment more toxic! We must confront the Jezzies in a Godly manner. We must take the high road no matter how much we don't want to. (And believe me, there will be times where you absolutely won't want to.)

Dealing with the Jezzies will require us to utilize the Honor Code of Conflict Resolution. Here's how it works:

1. Let the dust settle.

Conflict resolution can't happen in the midst of high emotions. We must give each other space and time to let the rawness of our emotions settle. Only then do we have a chance to heal the relationship and our hurt feelings.

This was a challenging step for me to apply. In the situation that resulted from the email referred to at the beginning of this chapter, the last thing I wanted to do was let the dust settle. I wanted to fix things – pronto! I wanted to prove my point and give all the reasons why I felt I was wronged! But that would not have helped. So instead, with the help of a Biblical counselor, all parties involved were given some guidelines to follow as we gave each other the space to let our raw emotions heal. The guidelines were simple: we could not talk about the situation to anyone for a specific amount of time, and we could not post cryptic messages on social media that could be misconstrued.

During this time, I wrote in my journal – a lot. In fact, several entries were rough draft letters written to the woman whose words had wounded me so deeply. I never actually gave her these letters, but they did serve a purpose. They provided a place for the hurt that was blistering inside of me to ooze out onto paper so I could get to the bottom of what I was really feeling.

When we burst through the door trying to prove our point, we end up saying words that we don't mean. These words always make the situation worse. Instead, we must be willing to give everyone involved the freedom to let their emotions settle. This can be difficult, but in the long run, it is vital to healing any relationship that has been damaged by the Jezzies.

2. Look in the mirror.

Take an honest assessment of your own habits, thoughts, and hidden hurts. Are there pockets of fear, insecurity, exhaustion, gossip, or even guilt in your own heart? If so, that's a sign that you've been dealing with a Jezzie either outwardly from another person or inwardly. Be brave enough to get real with yourself and recognize the things that need to be healed in your own heart first.

When I looked in the mirror and saw the reflection of my own heart in this situation, I was a bit surprised. Staring back at me was a giant dose of insecurity mixed with traces of guilt, blame, and even pride.

Insecurity...because leaders that I looked up to and wanted to be friends with had treated me poorly. I trusted them, but they spoke careless words of gossip behind my back. Eventually those words about my abilities and talents reached my ears, and it hurt. It also made me question and doubt the gifts and talents God had given me. I thought that these women were right because they had been placed in a position of leadership; therefore, their opinions must matter. I was wrong; I allowed their opinions to matter more than what God had told me. It was a tough road to walk, and for many months I wavered between trying to be confident in who God said I was and being totally insecure in the perception others had of me.

That's what insecurity does. It causes confusion and gets you so wrapped up in the opinions of others that the words of God seem miniscule in comparison to the idle words of people operating in the Jezzies.

Traces of guilt showed up, too. I walked around feeling guilty because I believed the lie that said, "Clearly you've done something so wrong that you should hang your head in shame!" Whenever guilt shows up, condemnation isn't too far behind. Condemnation is the thing that makes you feel a strong disapproval of something you've done before. Ever felt that way? It also makes you feel judged.

Now, clearly there is a difference between expressing disapproval in a manner that helps someone grow and expressing disapproval in a condescending way that ultimately leaves you feeling condemned and just plain...guilty. There is a difference! Guidance is necessary for growing and becoming spiritually mature; however, when God gives guidance, He does it by extending conviction - which leads to repentance and healing. It makes you feel free, light, better, whole. Condemnation leads to none of that and leaves us feeling worthless and empty. In my guilty, condemned state of mind, I was feeling all of those things.

Then there was the blaming. Oh, the blaming! In my very hurt state of being, I found myself blaming everyone else for making me feel so insecure, guilty, and condemned. But blaming others only made me feel, act, and look like a victim. Overcomers can never act like victims. Because they aren't! But there I was, blaming and walking around with a victim mentality. Ick.

Finally, pride reared its ugly head, too. Pride screamed, "I did nothing wrong to deserve this unfair treatment!" Pride kept me focused on the hurt and the injustice that I was experiencing. It stopped me from rising up and moving forward.

These were the Jezzies staring back at me when I finally found the courage to look in the mirror. I had to get vulnerable enough with myself to admit that they were there because only then could I do something about it. With a spirit of humility, I asked God to forgive me for entertaining these Jezzies and operating in them. Then I asked Him to clean out my heart and give me a fresh start.

That's what we all must do when we look in the mirror. I must warn you - it will be difficult. It will require vulnerability with the one person we usually all hide from the most – ourselves. But it will be worth it in every way. And it will open the door to the next step.

3. Extend grace and forgiveness.

On this journey of resolving conflict with honor, we must give each other the grace to share our feelings and get it out, knowing that we each have our reasons and excuses for why something happened. Grace allows us to hear the hurt, the reasons, the excuses, and not be damaged by it. Grace leads to forgiveness. And forgiveness is a choice, not a right. However, it is one each person must make for the relationship to be fully healed and restored.

I wish I could say that this step was applied in the situation with the women in leadership at my church. While it was applied on the part of myself and another person involved, the ones in leadership did not apply this one, nor did they apply the following steps. It's important to note, though, that this step is still important even if everyone involved doesn't do it. From a personal standpoint, the freedom that comes from walking through all five steps of the Honor Code of Conflict Resolution is worth every moment where it might be excruciating and painful.

While Step Three didn't happen with this particular situation, I do have an experience where it happened with a close childhood friend. At the same time that this friction was happening at church, one of my lifelong friendships was experiencing a similar situation. Living in different states had finally taken its toll on our friendship and we found ourselves growing apart, hurting each other in the process because we didn't confront the issues. Eventually we found ourselves head to head with the truth: we had been tolerating and operating in the Jezzies.

We applied Steps One and Two, and then we found ourselves getting to Step Three. We extended grace and forgiveness to each other. We allowed each other to share our hurts without judging each other, and we both asked for forgiveness for the ways we acted and the judgments that we had been holding on to. It was a beautiful experience that helped save our friendship. It also opened the door to moving forward with conflict resolution to Step Four...

4. Seek to understand the other person.

We must make the choice to try and understand the other person without casting judgment.

My lifelong friend and I had to get to the point of extending grace and forgiveness before we could begin to seek to understand each other. It took a long conversation where we asked tough questions of each other to be able to get through this process, but we came out on the other side with a newfound respect for each other. It was worth it.

Understanding the other person does not mean that you give up your convictions. It does not mean that you are weak. Quite the opposite actually. It takes a strong person to be able to take a step back and look at something from the other person's point of view without being judgmental. It takes an overcomer to do this. And it must be done if you're going to heal broken relationships that have been damaged by the Jezebel spirit.

Once we go through the process of letting the dust settle, looking in the mirror, extending grace and forgiveness, and seeking to understand the other person, we can move into the final step of conflict resolution: establishing new behaviors.

5. Establish new behaviors.

Moving forward will require each person to make an effort in following some basic friendship guidelines. If spending time together is important to one person, the other must make an effort to do that. If words of encouragement are important to one, then the other must make an effort, too. New habits may have to form, but it's necessary.

My lifelong friend and I agreed to stay in touch more often by scheduling chats on social media, skype dates, or simply making a point to reach out to each other more often with a text message. We made it a point to pay attention to each other's lives on social media by liking or commenting on pictures. We made a point to be present.

Establishing new behaviors will look different for everyone, but this is a vital step if the relationship is to be restored in any form.

~ TOXIC FRIENDSHIPS V. HEALTHY FRIENDSHIPS ~

The Honor Code of Conflict Resolution doesn't just work in friendships; it works across the board. However, it is especially handy for women when we experience problems with our girlfriends. Women are relational creatures, so it makes perfect sense that we would experience attacks from the Jezebel spirit in our friendships more than in any other area. Anytime these characteristics show up in a friendship, the relationship has the potential to turn toxic if these habits are not taken care of quickly.

Toxic, Jezebel spirit type habits and thought patterns show up in covert ways though, so it takes a trained eye to see them. For instance, in a recent study during one of our coaching programs with a group of young females, ninety-four percent of girls ages eleven to eighteen reported that they rarely or never lie to their friends. However, only seventeen percent of the same girls admitted that they are honest with their friends when their feelings have been hurt. That's a big difference! To the naked eye, this might seem harmless, but underneath it lay some very disturbing characteristics of the Jezebel spirit such as manipulation, lying, and distrust.

If we are going to be women who overcome, we must be willing to fix any discord in our friendships. Not only that, it's imperative that we also train up the generations of girlfriends after us in the same way. When we teach this to high school students in our coaching programs, we make sure to give them a glimpse of the qualifications for a toxic friendship, as well as a healthy friendship. I know, I know, it totally seems like we should be able to easily identify the differences in these types of friendships by now. I mean, we are adult women here. But toxic friendships can start as healthy ones and stealthily develop into toxic ones before we even realize it.

I encourage you to take a brief moment to read these descriptions, and do an assessment in your own life, of your own friendships.

Toxic Friendships:

A toxic friend is someone who makes you feel badly about yourself. She makes you feel like you don't belong, like you're not good enough, and she is toxic because she slowly kills the person you were designed to be with lies and labels. A toxic friend always operates in the Jezzies. Her true colors are displayed by the following habits:

- She gossips about you.
- She posts embarrassing pictures or words on social media about you to try to hurt you intentionally. (This can also be done in cryptic ways by posting about a situation but leaving out the names of those involved. And don't make the mistake of thinking that this only happens among teenagers. Oh no! Adult women can often be worse about this.)

- Shares your secrets with others and says, "It's no big deal! You need to loosen up!"
- Judges the way you look and the clothes you wear.
- Holds grudges against you.
- Breaks her promises to you and others.
- Belittles you and makes fun of you.
- Cares more about talking about herself and her problems and never lets you talk about things that matter to you.
- Betrays you.
- Makes everything into a competition and feels threatened or jealous if you do something better than she does.
- Finds fault in everything you do.

Healthy Friendships:

A Healthy Friend is someone who builds you up, encourages you, supports your dreams and the things you like to do! Her true colors show up in the following ways:

- She encourages you.
- Respects your feelings in person, when with others, and on the internet.
- Treats people the way she wants to be treated.
- Keeps your secrets.
- Keeps her promises.
- Supports you and stands by your side. Cheers you on when you feel overwhelmed or sad. She will sit with you in silence when you just need a friend to be there.
- She is honest with you and tells you how she feels in a way that honors you and strengthens your friendship.
- Spending time with a true friend makes you feel energized and happy, not drained and belittled.
- She shares and lets you share, too. It's not always about her!

- She doesn't compete with you, but she encourages you to be your best even if it means you are better than she is at something.
- She asks for forgiveness when she's done something hurtful, and she also forgives when her feelings have been hurt.

When we aren't free to be honest and vulnerable with our friends, we are letting the friendship thrive in a toxic environment. Vulnerability is a must for a healthy friendship to grow and strengthen! But it takes courage to face the fact that a once healthy relationship has grown toxic.

If you find yourself recognizing a toxic friendship right now, take some time to journal through what's happening and the feelings that have surfaced. Walk through the Honor Code of Conflict Resolution with the person involved, if possible. But be prepared – some friendships are so toxic that they won't be fixed until each party chooses to rise up and confront the hard issues, a.k.a. the Jezzies. If that happens, keep walking through the steps on your own with God so that you can keep growing as an overcomer.

•••

We've just spent a considerable amount of time learning about the Jezebel spirit, confronting the issues, and learning some skills to help us find the courage to resolve the conflict that ensues from this wretched spirit. As we end this chapter, my prayer for you is that you won't tolerate the Jezebels in your life anymore. Hold on to what you have in Christ! Repent and let him cleanse your soul.

The reward?

Intimacy of the highest level with the Creator of your soul. That's what is waiting for the woman who overcomes by courageously dealing with the Jezzies in her life.

...

Dear Jesus,

Forgive me for tolerating Jezebel in my life. Forgive me for being controlling, using manipulation, twisting your word, and thriving in rebellion. Forgive me for being self-centered and selfish, unteachable, arrogant, and condescending. Forgive me for placing blame and guilt on others. Forgive me for my pride and the constant feelings of seeking revenge. Clean my heart and make it new so I can experience a deeper relationship with you.

In Jesus' name, Amen

TRUTH ABOUT ME STATEMENTS:

- I refuse to operate in the behaviors of the Jezebel Spirit (a.k.a. the Jezzies).
- When someone hurts me, I will choose to forgive him or her.
- I have the courage to resolve conflict with honor.

PERSONAL REFLECTION TIME:

- Which characteristics of the Jezebel spirit have shown up in your life?
- How did those characteristics make you feel?
- From whom do you need to ask forgiveness?
- Whom do you need to forgive?

RELATED WORDS OF LIFE TO STUDY:

"The Lord does not look at the things people look at. People look at the outward appearance, but the Lord looks at the heart." ~1 Samuel 16:7 NIV

"Therefore, there is now no condemnation for those who are in Christ Jesus." ~Romans 8:1

"Then every church will know that appearances don't impress me. I x-ray every motive." ~Revelation 2:23, *The Message*

"Don't copy the behavior and customs of this world, but let God transform you into a new person by changing the way you think. Then you will learn to know God's will for you, which is good and pleasing and perfect." ~Romans 12:2 NLT

6

She is Wanted!

~courage to be authentic~

The purple wand slid through each strand of hair as the stylist combed it into my dark brown bangs. At the tender age of seven, my little heart was bursting with excitement over the fact that Mom said it was okay to get this vibrant streak of color put in my hair. It was only temporary, of course. Within a few days it would wash right out. Still, my heart was filled with pride, and I felt so authentically me in that moment. Purple hair and all.

Several years later I watched in admiration as an older friend in youth group daringly colored her own hair into a vibrant shade of maroon. She was so brave! The color represented her spunky personality so well. Part of me wished that I could find the courage to do that. Imagine – me – with maroon hair! I had long forgotten about the days of purple bangs from my childhood. Somewhere along the way, I buried that part of me. Maybe it was the fact that we had moved a few times, and I was now known as "the new girl." Or maybe the labels that were placed on kids who were brave enough to express themselves rang so loudly in my head that I dared not to put myself in a position of having those labels attached to me, too. Whatever it was, a part of me was buried and as the years went on, the distance between my authentic self and the woman in the mirror became as far away as the sun is from the earth.

It's funny how something as simple as the color of your hair can be an indicator of whether or not you are living authentically as the woman God made you to be. It takes courage to be real...and many times we hide from it because we feel like we won't be wanted if people know the real us. We fear that our realness won't be good enough. But what is "good enough" anyway? Who even determines that? Striving to be "good enough" was never part of God's plan for us. Often when we live with the desire of meeting everyone else's expectations of us, we miss the bigger purpose God has for us.

•••

"I see right through your work. You have a reputation for vigor and zest, but you're dead, stone-dead."

Believe it or not, this is not a line from a movie. Kinda sounds like it though, right? I mean, I can just imagine some hero saying these words in a stern voice with searing eyes that glare at the enemy. "You're dead, stone-dead." It would be awesome if this was a line from the next super-hero action movie. But it's not. It's from the Bible, and there's some rich wisdom coming our way as we continue through this text.

Let's read on...

"Up on your feet! Take a deep breath! Maybe there's life in you yet. But I wouldn't know it by looking at your busywork; nothing of GOD's work has been completed. Your condition is desperate. Think of the gift you once had in your hands, the Message you heard with your ears – grasp it again and turn back

to God.

If you pull the covers back over your head and sleep on, oblivious to God, I'll return when you least expect it, break into your life like a thief in the night.

You still have a few followers of Jesus in Sardis who haven't ruined themselves wallowing in the muck of the world's ways. They'll walk with me on parade! They've proved their worth!

Conquerors will march in the victory parade, their names indelible in the Book of Life. I'll lead them up and present them by name to my Father and his Angels. Are your ears awake? Listen. Listen to the Wind Words, the Spirit blowing through the churches." ~Revelation 3:1-6, MSG

The people in this passage have a reputation of vigor and zest. That means they are known for having energy, liveliness, and a spirit of animation. They look and act healthy and strong. Yet, their reputation doesn't fool God because He calls them dead. Stone dead. He knows the truth of what is hiding in their hearts, regardless of the vigor and zest that seem to be there. Did you know that it's entirely possible to be completely alive in the physical sense that you laugh, you have fun from time to time, you talk and move and do everything that equates to life, yet feel dead on the inside? This is a real thing; it's an epidemic really. There are people all around you – maybe you're even one of them – who have experienced this feeling and lived this sad reality.

~ DISTRACTED BY DESPERATE BUSYWORK ~

Several years ago I found myself wondering, *"Is this all there is to life?"* Oh, I kept busy every day with a job that I liked most days, even loved from time to time. As the Event Planner at a hotel, I was up to my eyeballs being busy with endless networking events and fun weddings. I was also involved with music ministry and was the Women's Event Coordinator at our church. There's no doubt I was busy all the time. But I had this nagging sense that there was something I was missing, something that I was born to do and wasn't doing. I was bored and yet constantly trying to measure up at the same time. I felt as though nothing of God's work had been completed, just like the verse in Revelation describes. There was this deep feeling inside that kept nudging me, making me feel as though I had missed the plans God had for me because I was just too...busy.

Yes, I read my Bible. Sometimes. Usually every Sunday at church and then it sat on my nightstand collecting dust the rest of the week. At least I knew where it was! I listened to mostly Christian music so I reasoned that at least I was getting truth on a daily basis in that way. Still, with all of these Christian habits, I felt dead inside. There was no excitement in my relationship with God because I didn't leave any room for it.

Don't get me wrong; I wasn't depressed...yet. I laughed a lot and smiled constantly. I was healthy and energetic for the most part. I had family and friends around me often. I just wasn't...fully living. I was stuck in a groundhog's day type of life where nothing exciting happened, nothing out of the ordinary. Just get up and go to work on Monday – repeat four times – spend the weekend watching television and going to church on Sunday and napping and then – repeat it all again. Alive in body. Going through the motions. A smile here, a giggle there, but dead in spirit.

All of the adventure and bravery had been sucked out of my life and instead happened only through the big box sitting on our entertainment center, and the idea of being an overcomer only existed in the movies.

Maybe you can relate?

I love how earlier in these verses it says, "Your condition is desperate." Yep. Pretty much! I was desperate for a life that was exciting and filled with God's miracles every day! I was desperate to know my purpose in life. I was desperate for more and yearning to find the courage to be one-hundred percent authentic so I could live the life I was designed for – the calling that was just waiting to burst forth from the depths of my soul.

~FINDING MY PURPOSE ~

One Friday afternoon, I found myself sitting with the hotel sales team at a leadership seminar. My boss had made sure that everyone who wanted to go could be there, and as the Event Planner, I figured it would be a great networking experience. Little did I know that the entire day would be a divine encounter to get me started on the courageous path of finding my purpose.

There were several amazing speakers lined up for the day; however, the one who caught my attention and connected with my soul the most was John Maxwell. He spoke about many topics that day, such as the fact that talent alone won't cut it; you must be willing to get the skills and attitudes necessary to use with the talent. That was a novel idea to me, and it totally rocked my world! He also spoke about our purpose and calling. The entire time, my pen scrambled to keep up with my thoughts as I caught the wisdom that spewed forth from his mouth. With every stroke of my pen, a spark lit in the depths of my soul. By the end of the day, the embers that had cooled in my heart over the years were rekindled, and a red-hot burning fire rose up inside.

That day – sitting with my coworkers in a leadership seminar - I felt God knocking on the doorway of my heart to step out in faith and trust Him with the unknown. The desire was so strong, that I took the risk. I started climbing the foggy staircase of personal growth and walking by faith without seeing the next step. I bought my first personal growth books that day and began actually reading them instead of letting them collect dust on my shelf. I started journaling more and listening to leadership podcasts. I began to open up my heart to long buried dreams again and pressed on, grasping the Message God had given me, and I decided to never look back. Because that's what overcomers do. When we recognize the path that leads to our calling, we reach out and grab it with everything we've got!

Finding my purpose didn't happen over night. It took many

nights, months, and to be one-hundred percent honest – years. It was an in depth journey of digging deep into the hidden, buried areas of my heart. Tough questions had to be answered, such as:

- If I could wake up tomorrow and not worry about any responsibilities or money, what would I do with my life?
- What did I dream of doing when I was kid?
- What are the things people are always telling me that I am good at, and how do those qualities fit with my dreams?
- What do I want my life legacy to be?
- Where do I want to travel?
- What experiences do I want to have?
- How do I really want to be spending my free time?
- What would I say and do if I wasn't afraid of what people would think of me?
- What are the things that are important to me?
- What am I willing to give up so I can live my life authentically?

These were the tough questions that filled up pages upon pages of my journals. At first, the answers to these questions were very superficial. Which makes a lot of sense because when we begin the journey of awakening the dreams that we've spent years hiding from, we've got to tiptoe around a bit because our mental and emotional muscles won't be strong enough to handle the enormity of it all. As I kept digging, the answers became easier to find. The dreams that had been buried began to resurface again, and a renewed passion was lit within my soul. I even discovered that some of those buried dreams had grown and were now bigger than they had ever been!

If you and I were having coffee together right now, I'd probably look at you after sharing this story, and with a glimmer in my eye and tenderness in my voice, ask you some very important questions. Since we aren't face to face, let's take the next few moments to pretend that these pages are a personal letter from me to you, okay? Here are a few questions that I would like to ask you, my friend:

When is the last time you allowed yourself to dream? When is the last time you wrote down some goals for what your year would look like? When is the last time you felt the pure joy of having accomplished something you set out to do?

If you don't know, then it would be wise to take some time and begin finding your purpose. Answer the questions from the previous page with vulnerability and no judgment toward yourself. Shut the door on the excuses and just allow yourself to dream again. It matters! It matters to God, and it matters to the people around you whether they realize it or not. You are wanted! YOU! Your life has a purpose and you must find it and live it out with everything you've got. There is something you were designed for that won't get accomplished unless you rise up and do it. Something that matters to God and His Kingdom. It's that important!

Now, I know. This whole experience can sometimes be a bit daunting, especially if you've never gone down this path before. Take a deep breath, my friend, you're not alone. To help you along the way, here are some of my favorite resources:

- *Chazown* – a book by Craig Groeschel that takes you on a journey of finding your purpose. It's a great resource that I highly suggest for any of my coaching clients struggling with this topic.
- *GEMS™*– a DVD study by Dani Johnson on personalities. It teaches you how to live authentically and communicate better with different personality types. It is an amazing resource for living authentically! You can get it at www.danijohnson.com.

My professional recommendation is for you to start with the book, *Chazown,* and then move on to the DVD study by Dani Johnson after that. Give yourself permission to go as fast or as slow as you need to with these resources. God has some important words of life to share with you as you discover your purpose; don't be so focused on getting through it all that you miss the rich wisdom He is waiting to share with you.

~ GET UP ON YOUR FEET! ~

A funny thing happens when you begin to find your purpose. It suddenly becomes impossible to do nothing! I don't mean it becomes impossible to rest; no, everything we discussed in Chapter Three still applies. However, it does become impossible to stay in the stagnant, desperate condition that you found yourself in prior to finding your purpose. Suddenly your eyes are open to the truth: You are WANTED! You have a divine calling on your life and it's time to wake up, get up on your feet, and live it! Once you have been awakened to that truth, it's hard to ignore it.

Yet, I feel it's my moral obligation to be real with you here. There will be days when you feel...unqualified. It's part of the journey. There will be moments where you begin to compare yourself to others. That's a trap designed to slow you down and eventually stop you! However, it can also be a very good compass, confirming the fact that you're on the right path. Whenever comparison rears its ugly head, take it as a sign that what you're about to do, or what you are doing, matters more than you realize. In spiritual terms, it's war!

The enemy uses comparison to bind you up and make you feel unworthy of the calling that God has placed on your life. And when you begin to find your purpose, the enemy gets mad. You see, when you're far away from your purpose, totally distracted with busywork and the things that don't matter, the enemy doesn't have to work very hard at all. He already knows that you're spiritually asleep, if not dead. But when you wake up from his mind controlling slumber – watch out! Suddenly the enemy is on high alert because you've escaped! So he works on overtime to try and capture you again, and he does this with comparison.

So don't be fooled. Instead, get up on your feet and keep going! Don't wallow or waste time comparing yourself to others. You don't know the assignment, the calling, the purpose that has been placed on the lives of those you're comparing yourself to. You know YOUR purpose. Your calling. Your unique assignment. Stay focused on that. When you wake up from your spiritual slumber that kept you spiritually dead inside, remember the words of Revelation 3:1-6, and hold on to them:

"Up on your feet! Take a deep breath! ...
Think of the gift you once had in your hands, the Message you heard with your ears – grasp it again and turn back to God...
Conquerors will march in the victory parade, their names indelible in the Book of Life. I'll lead them up and present them by name to my Father and his Angels. Are your ears awake? Listen. Listen to the Wind Words, the Spirit blowing through the churches." ~Revelation 3:1-6, MSG

Never forget that you are an overcomer. If you weren't, you wouldn't be reading this book. When comparison attacks, remember who you are. Remember *whose* you are. Remember your purpose. Remember that you are wanted – spiritually alive – and that you now have the courage to live authentically, so get up on your feet and do it!

~ SO I GOT A TATOO ~

On a personal note, I must confess that there are moments where I'm still peeling back the deeper layers of my authenticity. It's a journey, and when we've lived the majority of our lives trying to hide from who we are, it takes a bit longer to uncover it all. I've learned to give myself grace as some of the characteristics of who I am still need time to develop. And that's okay. It's part of God's brilliant plan for my life, and I've learned to trust His process.

However, I've also learned to give myself permission just to be real. That's what we've got to do when we go down this path – release ourselves from all expectations of perfectionism. Just. Be. Real.

So I got a tattoo. I already know it won't be my last.

I'm not sure how that sits with you, but I'm just being totally vulnerable and authentic with you, so I see no need to hide it. I used to think that tattoos were something I should never get. I made up a ton of excuses and was very judgmental toward anyone who had one. I see now that this attitude was really just a means of self-protection because deep down inside, expressing myself with words of life on a tattoo is an authentic thing for me. It's as authentic as the purple bangs I loved as a kid. I just didn't know it back then. So I judged.

Until one day…I didn't.

The more I became okay with being authentic, the more I found myself trying to understand other people, too. That happens along the way as well – you become totally in love with who God made you to be, and suddenly you want to understand others without judgment. It's a beautiful process!

So I started asking people with tattoos what made them get them in the first place. What did the artwork or the words mean to them? I found out that almost everyone had a significant meaning behind their tattoos. Some of them had significant dates or the names of loved ones imprinted on them. Others had symbols. Yes, there were some who had decided to get tattoos without thinking, and they had absolutely no meaning; maybe they even regretted them. But for the most part, it was a deeply meaningful way of expressing something that mattered to them.

After going through our apartment fire, and the health challenges that I'll be sharing in an upcoming chapter, I decided it was time to be real with myself and no longer hide my authenticity. So I got a tattoo.

It's on the inside of my right foot, and it simply says, "Walk by faith." It also has two little footprints after the words. (Not very many people ask, but the footprints are in memory of a baby that we miscarried during that season.) Other people might think it's a horrible thing to do to a person's body – ink it up. I, however, think that my tattoo is a beautiful reminder of the faith that was developed during a treacherous season of deep pain and uncertainty.

My best friends and I have plans to get matching tattoos that say, "Be Brave." I love words of life, and so I'm pretty sure that any other tattoos I get will always have words that mean a lot to me on them. However, as my authenticity grows, I'm giving myself permission to change my mind, and this confession is in no way a binding, legal contract!

~ THE COURAGE TO BE AUTHENTIC ~

We've been focusing in this chapter on the truth that you are wanted by God and that it will require all of your courage to rise up and live authentically. You can do it because, remember, you were born to overcome. And those who are known as overcomers grab hold of their purpose in life and never let go. Busywork doesn't distract them; they stay focused on God's work. They say goodbye to that stone-dead mundane life, take a deep breath, and jump into the unknown. Overcomers walk by faith because they trust the One who has called them. They rise up when others choose to sleep. They stand for truth when others wallow in the muck of confusion – truth of who they are, who others are, and most of all, God's truth. They march on in victory because they never give up. Never give in.

It's no accident that you're here, reading these words. You are WANTED! Spiritually dead or alive! The courage to be authentic is already IN you, waiting to be activated. If it weren't, these words would not be tugging at your heart right now.

As you walk forward, courageously authentic, never lose sight of the truth that God loves you. He brought you to this page just as you are because He wants nothing more than to help you walk in the authority of the overcomer that you were born to be; the overcomer that you are. If you're spiritually alive, He wants you to thrive and keep doing His work. Go deeper even! If you're spiritually dead, He wants to revive you so that you can fully experience life as He designed it for you – before it's too late. Because one day, it will be too late.

You were born to be an overcomer. A conqueror. Victorious with your name written in the Book of Life – your name presented and acknowledged before God and His angels. That's your purpose!

The question is: will you rise up on your feet and grasp it, or will you pull back the covers and sleep on? I believe there's life in you yet, Overcomer.

Rise up!

•••

Dear Jesus,

Forgive me for going through the motions. I want to grab hold of everything you have for me! I desire to live the life you've planned for me! I invite you into my life again and give you permission to ignite a passion in my soul. No more groundhog's day. No more snoozing through life, wondering if there's more. Jesus, I'm ready to be revived and set free as the overcomer you've destined me to be!

In Jesus' Name, Amen

TRUTH ABOUT ME STATEMENTS:

- I have been revived and set free!
- The calling on my life is good enough because God says it is. He is the Qualifier and He says I am qualified!
- I have been equipped with everything I need to accomplish the calling God has placed on my life.

PERSONAL REFLECTION TIME:

- Would you consider yourself spiritually alive in Christ, or have you grown spiritually dead, just going through the motions?
- What does "turning back to God" look like for you?
- What "busywork" have you allowed to overtake you?
- If you're not living the life God ultimately designed for you, what does that look like? What dream has been buried in your heart and how could you dig it up and use it for God's glory?
- Take some time to journal through the questions in the "Finding My Purpose" section and ask God for wisdom and discernment as you do.

RELATED WORDS OF LIFE TO STUDY:

"When God lives and breathes in you (and he does, as surely as he did in Jesus), you are delivered from that dead life." ~Romans 8:11, *The Message*

"Therefore, if anyone is in Christ, he is a new creation; the old has gone, the new has come!" ~2 Corinthians 5:17, NIV

"For we are God's workmanship, created in Christ Jesus to do good works, which God prepared in advance for us to do." ~Ephesians 2:10, NIV

"But because of his great love for us, God, who is rich in mercy, made us alive with Christ even when we were dead in transgressions - it is by grace you have been saved." ~Ephesians 2:4-5, NIV

"For I know the plans I have for you, declares the Lord, plans to prosper you and not to harm you, plans to give you hope and a future." ~Jeremiah 29:11, NIV

7

She Faces Lies & Labels

~courage to face fears~

Anticipation and a healthy dose of anxiety trickled through our bodies as we welcomed the handful of women that would fill the room for our first coaching program. Raychel and I had dreamed of this moment for years, and here it was, right in front of us. God's promises had come full circle, and we watched in awe as the reality of our dreams unfolded before our eyes.

Raychel stepped up to the front of the room to welcome the ladies, and as she did, removed her jacket to reveal what was written in black and red marker on her white t-shirt. A hush fell over the crowd as the unsuspecting women began to read the horrible words:

Fear. Depression. Rejection. Mean. Unworthy. Poor. A big red "A."

With grace in her step and determination in her heart, she began to share the lies and labels that had been a part of her story since childhood. In her teenage years, Raychel experienced what it was like to have her family fall apart. When her dad left her mom and filed for a divorce, she took on the label of abandoned. Fear attached itself to her as well, and she began to believe the lie that she would one day be destined to walk in the footsteps of her parents' divorce.

As an adult, Raychel found the labels only grew, not diminished. When she began looking for love from someone other than her husband, because her marriage was going through a challenging season, she painted a big red "A" on her heart for adultery. When she experienced postpartum depression during and after her pregnancies, anxiety trailed behind her, dragging her further into the pit of despair. Out of that anxiety grew the belief that she was a bad mom and a crazy nut job.

When she finally found the courage to overcome the lies of her past, and determined to do something amazing with her life and career, the word "prideful" was suddenly thrown at her from trusted colleagues and loved ones. It became impossible for her to be confident, healthy, and whole while she held on to all of these excuses, lies, and labels!

But Raychel Chumley is an overcomer.

She recognized the painful process that she needed to go through to discover the truth and say goodbye to the lies and labels forever. By practicing new skills and thought patterns, she found the courage to confront her fears. She learned to dream again and began to believe that God had huge plans for her life. In her own words, "I had to see myself as the beautiful daughter He created me to be. I had to be okay with the truth that I wasn't a bad mom - I was a survivor. I had to allow Him to erase the BIG RED "A" and all the other lies and labels I wore."

This is part of the recipe that creates an overcomer. It takes a pinch of bravery, mixed in with a plentiful scoop of vulnerability, and a spoonful of strength. This recipe calls for the rejection of lies and labels. Only then can you believe the truth so the beautiful authenticity of the overcomer that you are, uncovered in the last chapter, can be revealed.

•••

According to dictionary.com, courage is defined as "the quality of mind or spirit that enables a person to face difficulty, danger, pain, etc., without fear; bravery." In the last two chapters we have journeyed through Chapters Two and Three in the book of Revelation for some wisdom on how to find the courage to resolve conflict and be authentic. I don't know about you, but the rich content provided in those scriptures has seriously rocked my world already. I'm trusting that a similar experience is happening for you, too.

However, it would be unwise to dive into the topic of courage in this section of the book without also bringing up the topic of fear. The two go hand in hand, and for that reason, in this chapter we will be taking a break again from the book of Revelation so we can cover this topic of fear that so many people wrestle with daily.

~ FACING THE FEARS OF LIES & LABELS ~

Raychel isn't the only one who has battled with lies and labels. In fact, on the evening of our very first group coaching event, we discovered a very important truth: we all have buried lies and labels written on our hearts that we've been, at times, too afraid to confront.

For instance, my own personal lies and labels bear the following words:

Snobby rich girl. Ashamed. Sick girl. Too skinny. Selfish. Hated. Not good enough. Ugly Fido. Not a leader. Always left out. Fearful. Depressed. Anxious. Goody two shoes. Lonely. I don't matter.

When I was a child, my parents were blessed to build their dream home in a small town. It was a beautiful home, and a big one. Our quaint family of three now had a very modern home complete with almost four-thousand square feet and six televisions. For some reason it was the talk of the town and I suddenly became labeled the snobby, rich, only child who got everything she wanted. That wasn't true. I was neither snobby nor did I get everything I ever wanted. However, I let the label be branded on my heart and began to feel ashamed because people who didn't know me thought something that wasn't true.

Being diagnosed with cystic fibrosis automatically gave me a stigma of "sick girl," whether I liked it or not. That wasn't true either. In fact, God's word tells us that He is the Healer and will heal all of our diseases. Yet, part of me believed this label and buried it deep down inside.

The other labels I carried around inside came from various places throughout my life. Kids calling me names when I wore a sweatshirt that said "Fido Dido," adult women feeling insecure and telling me that I should never consider myself a leader, my own insecurities screaming words of fear, depression, and anxiety during seasons of trials and deep pain. The labels we brand ourselves with aren't always put there by other people; many times we singe the words on our hearts ourselves because we fear digging deep enough to find the truth behind the lies.

The ladies in our coaching group that evening discovered their own lies and labels, too. And when they stepped back and surveyed the words written around the room on giant sticky notes attached to the wall, they were all amazed. Many of them had no idea that others struggled with the same lies and labels. They thought they were the only ones – all alone, stranded on a deserted island of insecurities, lies, labels, and fears.

~ FEAR STRIVES TO ISOLATE AND SILENCE ~

What are the lies, labels, and fears that have been branded on your heart and buried deep within? Whatever they are, allow me to be the one to let you know that you're not alone. Every single person on earth battles with lies and labels from time to time, some more than others. Fear's goal is to make you believe that you are the only one who battles with these insecurities because when you believe that lie, you'll stay silent.

It's time to make some noise.

From this point forward, fear no longer has the upper hand in your life. Why? Because you were born to overcome it. You have the persistency and courage of an overcomer and today we're going to rise up and say goodbye to the isolation and silence that fear has been keeping you hostage under for years.

In my first self-published book, *In Sickness and In Health: Lessons Learned on the Journey from Cystic Fibrosis to Total Health,* I gave some insight into fear. Here's what I shared:

"Fear is such a silly thing really. It's sneaky and it keeps us stuck. Fear keeps us sick or keeps us from moving forward into a healthier version of ourselves by tricking us into thinking that we are being 'careful' when really we're just being fearful. Fear likes to mask the truth. It clouds our mind so we can't see any other possible outcomes other than bad ones.

But here's what fear doesn't want us to know: fear can serve as a compass. In fact, it's the best compass out there! If there's something you've always dreamed of doing but you're afraid of it, then you MUST do it because waiting on the other side of that fear is something that will equip you for your future.

Fear is conquered by faith; faith is usually sharpened by tribulations and trials. In fact, in the Bible we are told to rejoice in trials and tribulations because the testing of our faith produces perseverance." (Mandy B. Anderson, *In Sickness And In Health,* 2011)

In the next chapter we will dive into the topic of faith and uncover some truths from the book of Revelation again. But while we are on this topic of fear and courage, let's take a moment to hear one woman's story of the fears she has faced. Maybe you can identify with the story this courageous woman recently shared in response to a devotional I wrote on my blog:

"I just finished re-reading chapter one and spent some time talking to myself about my fears. It was interesting to me that all my fears involve physical pain. I am not afraid of death because I know God; I am not afraid of failure because I can only move up from being homeless two years ago. I am however afraid of being raped, molested, or physically hurt by someone.

These fears stem from a lot of issues in my past. But as I was praying and understanding these fears, God spoke to me. He said, "I will protect you." And in my heart I know that even if these things did happen to me, I would survive, because I am a fighter, I have before and I will continue to.

I sat a while and thought about whether or not to share this, but if there is one thing I have learned, its that fear wants us to stay silenced. I don't leave the house alone with my daughter, pretty much ever, my husband or friends or mother is usually always with me, because I am so overcome with fear of someone trying to hurt us, and what might happen if I cant fight back for her... yup. I don't leave the house after dark, no matter how much I need ink, or milk, or anything because I am overcome with fear of walking to my car. So I know its time for change. I want my life back..."

This brave mom took the first step – she spent time allowing herself to feel her fears, and asked God to show her where they stemmed from. As she did, He began to set her free. She also recognized the importance of finding the courage to be weak for the purpose of eventually growing stronger.

~ COURAGE TO BE WEAK ~

It was only three years ago that I sat at the kitchen table, my cup of triple venti soy caramel machiatto resting in my hands as I expressed my feelings to my close friends.

"Yes, I'm okay – but lately I've been really tired and getting over being sick. It's kind of lonely when Nate is gone for work, and

I know I seem like a go-getter, but lately I feel more depressed and end up doing nothing and feeling like no one notices me because they're all living their lives while I just sit at home tired..."

My friends let me spew my emotions as they looked at me with sincere interest and concern. Over the last few years leading up to this conversation, these two women had watched me overcome cystic fibrosis; they watched me rise above the emotional stress of PTSD from losing my home to a fire; they rejoiced with me as my marriage grew stronger, and we paid off debt; they supported my dreams. On this particularly dreary day, they understood the need for me to talk out my emotions and the pain that had been building up since my miscarriage a few months earlier. After several minutes of me sharing my thoughts, Madison looked at me and with piercing eyes said the most freeing words I had heard all week, "Mandy, you know it's all right if you're not okay, right?"

Before I could process what was said, I found myself mechanically saying, "Yes, I know. I'm okay, really!"

That's when Raychel piped in with a look of skeptical compassion on her face, "It sounds like you're really not, Sweetie."

Stunned at the reality of what was unfolding before me, I closed my mouth and replayed my words. It was true. I wasn't okay, and I was denying myself the opportunity to receive that fact.

I thanked them for their honesty and gave them permission to point out the truth anytime I might be blinded to it. After all, how else would I grow and overcome things if I didn't even realize what was hindering me? That night I went home and got brutally honest with myself, and with God.

It's so easy to stuff our feelings and emotions in a place where we don't see them. Human nature is to ignore them and pretend they don't exist. The problem with this is that our bodies still feel the stress even if our minds refuse to let us process it. Emotions can make you sick, and lies, labels, and fears will always keep you stuck if you don't find the courage to persist in getting to the truth.

As I allowed my emotions to surface in the pitch black dark of night, and I felt the intensity of them, the following truths about courage and weakness were revealed to me:

1. It takes courage to feel your emotions and face the lies and labels.

Most people will not feel their emotions, nor will they confront their lies, labels, and fears. The intensity of them becomes overwhelming and the truth often too much to bear. Crying, anger, and sadness are often looked upon as characteristics of the weak. That, my friend, is a big fat lie. The truth is that feeling your emotions makes you stronger. Facing the lies and labels strengthens you. It helps you heal and process the circumstances in your life. In your moments of weakness, the God of All mankind can come in and strengthen you - if you let Him. Feeling your emotions takes courage.

2. It takes courage to be vulnerable with yourself and others.

All I know is that when I'm vulnerable with myself, and others, the shackles of stress fall off and my boldness returns. Faith returns. Strength grows. Vulnerability opens the doors to overcoming the pain and chaos that has kept us blinded. It allows us to rise up out of the ashes of our circumstances!

Being vulnerable also encourages others when they walk through similar seasons. People need to see that they aren't alone. They are yearning for authenticity from others who have made it through chaos and pain so they, too, can find the hope to do the same! So don't shy away from being vulnerable. Embrace it!

3. It takes courage to admit when you are weak.

Putting on a brave mask, while hiding from the root problem day in and day out is exhausting. It is! You get stuck in a mind-numbing, never-ending cycle that wears you down until you are left with hopelessness, more fear, and sometimes, even sickness. The mask might make you look strong to others, but on the inside you are terrified, weak, and frail. It takes far more courage to admit the truth than to keep hiding from it and pretending to be strong. It takes courage to rise up and say, "Enough is enough!"

Maybe you're in a position of weakness right now, and you've been denying yourself the ability to not be okay. If so, it's all right. I give you permission to cry. I give you permission to be angry and feel the sadness and pain so you can release it effectively. Life is a journey, and courage is birthed out of weakness and vulnerability. In fact, God tells us in 2 Corinthians 12:9-10 that His power is made perfect in our weakness. When we are weak, it gives Him the chance to be strong!

So you see, my friend, it really is all right if you're not okay right now. Receive that fact, and some day soon, you will be okay again. Recognize that there is a deep refinement that happens when you find the courage to admit that you're weak.

~ I THOUGHT I WAS STRONGER ~

In my own journey of overcoming fears and healing from PTSD and anxiety, certain situations or experiences seem to pick open the scab and the bleeding slowly starts again. Many times I don't even notice the trail until it's too late; frustration, anger, a sudden deep sense of sorrow, extreme fatigue, and even episodes of fear slowly seep out of the wound before I'm aware of what's happening. Have you ever experienced this?

In the coaching and counseling world, the situations or experiences that result in those feelings are called triggers. Triggers can be anything from certain seasons of the year, to smells, or even material objects. When you've struggled with fear, depression, anxiety, PTSD, or any other emotional traumas, triggers will come up. They threaten your peace and can derail your progress when you're not aware of them. That's why we must learn to recognize, identify, and even anticipate our triggers. It's an important part of overcoming fears, lies, and labels.

I have found that my ability to recognize the seasons that trigger those feelings in my own life has strengthened over the years. Through experience, I have developed an ability to anticipate my own triggers and therefore equip myself to overcome them, or at the very least, identify them quicker in hindsight and extend grace to myself.

Maybe you'd like to discover how to do that, too?

A few years after the fire, I found myself visiting my parents for the weekend. On more than one occasion I drove past the location where our home once stood. The apartment had been rebuilt, and for the first time I could look at it and almost smile. Almost. On the last day there, I ended up driving past the apartment building with Ajah B. sitting on my passenger seat, and all the memories of that horrible experience flooded back into my mind. I could see myself driving down the road trying to reach the building filled with sky high flames; I could sense the sickening feeling in my stomach as I imagined my precious fur baby dying in the fire; and then I could sense the peace and overwhelming gratitude when I held her in my arms again after six hours of believing she was gone. Almost three years later these feelings were still so fresh, and yet...this time I could appreciate the broken road that we traveled to get to where we are today. I wouldn't want to relive it, but I wouldn't take it back either. All these things went through my mind as I drove out of town and headed home.

Later that night I called my husband to let him know that I had made it home. He was working out of town, and we decided to talk again before we both went to sleep so I could finish unpacking and get my treatments done. Around 10:45 PM I tried calling Nate again and it went straight to voicemail. Since this isn't uncommon in the areas that he travels, I also sent a text message. Ten minutes later I still had not heard from him. Over the next two hours I tried several more times to reach him with no success.

That's when the panic settled in. I was already exhausted from a busy weekend and traveling, so my ability to reign in my emotions and think with a level head was comatose. I spent the rest of the night wondering where my husband was and worrying about the phone ringing to tell me there was an accident and he was gone.

Triggers often hit without warning, especially when we are still learning to identify them. This was one of those times. Looking back now, I can clearly see what set me off. My trigger that day was the apartment building. The finger that pulled the trigger was exhaustion, and the bullet of worry, fear, and anxiety hit its target right on: my mind and fragile emotions.

I'm not even going to tell you how many times I called my husband and texted him. It's embarrassing.

The next morning, after four hours of sleep, I woke at 5:30 A.M. to discover that there was still no message from him. At that point I started telling God that I was NOT ready for any more pain or loss. I told him that I was just getting to the point of getting back to a new "normal," and I couldn't handle any more heartbreak at this point of my journey.

It was only after this confession that I was able to grab my Bible, focus on God's truth, and face the fact that no matter what pain comes my way, I can, in fact, get through it.

There's something powerful that happens when we confess our fears. It doesn't make us weak; it makes us stronger. It helps us see ourselves clearly, and it's through our confession that we allow God to work fully in our lives and through our situations.

In that moment I was reminded that God always hears us, even when it seems He doesn't. I was reminded that God always carries us through, even when we don't see Him working. I was reminded that sometimes emotions and fatigue are too much for us to bear alone and we must fall into the arms of God for peace, rest, and restoration.

Ten minutes after I immersed myself in God's word, I tried calling Nate again. This time he answered, and I broke down in tears. I was so happy to hear his voice, so embarrassed by my overreaction, and so utterly exhausted, that I just lost it. He had fallen asleep and somehow his phone had turned to "emergency only" calls, so nothing was getting through. He apologized and we came up with a plan to make sure that I don't overreact again in the future. I hung up the phone and crawled back into bed where I slept for another four hours.

If you're struggling with PTSD, anxiety, or fear today because of a traumatic event in your life or some sort of sickness, I pray that this encourages you. You are not alone. Give yourself some grace. Journal about your feelings so you can find out what your triggers are. Share your hurts with a trusted friend, spouse, or counselor so that you can grow from your pain. You were never meant to set up camp in the valley of despair and fear. You're just passing through!

~ CONFRONTING THE FEAR ~

Recognizing our triggers and overcoming them won't happen without first confronting our fears. After walking through this in my own life and helping clients overcome similar circumstances, I've learned that there is an actual method to this process. However, it is not a one-time fix it type thing; it must be applied every time fear pops in. Let's end our focus today with three steps to confronting your fears.

1. Feel It and Confess It

Crazy as it sounds, we must feel the fear to its very core. As we've mentioned before, most people ignore their fears and just stuff them down further. That won't help you overcome it! Give yourself permission to find the courage to feel it. Journal about it, cry about it, scream over it...whatever you have to do to let it all out, do it. Hiding and ignoring it will just make it grow and give it more power. So feel it – be honest enough and brave enough to look it in the eyes and stare it down.

Take it one step further after you've felt it and confess your fears out loud. When we keep our fears in our thoughts, all we do is marinade in more fear. Confess it out loud! Once a fear is expressed out loud, our ears hear how silly it sounds, and our problem-solving skills start to kick in. There is power in confessing that you're afraid of something, yet you're going to choose to overcome it anyway. No more fake bravery! Feel it and confess it.

2. Speak with Authority

Proverbs 18:21 tells us that our tongues have the power of life and death and we will eat the fruit of them. Our words have power! In Luke 10:19, we are told that we have been given the authority to overcome ALL the powers of the enemy. That includes the power to overcome...

- fearful thoughts
- scary thoughts
- doubtful thoughts
- worry-filled thoughts
- suicidal thoughts
- thoughts of depression
- thoughts of anxiety
- thoughts of insignificance
- thoughts of intimidation
- thoughts of abandonment
- thoughts of sickness
- thoughts of rejection

The list goes on and on, but the fact remains that we have been given the authority – through the power of the Holy Spirit and the blood of Jesus Christ – to trample over all of the traps that the enemy sets for us.

In case you haven't picked up on it yet, our thoughts are the birthplace of our fears. We can't always choose the thoughts that pop into our brains, but we can choose how we respond to them.

Speaking with authority is one of the best ways to snatch our fears and kick them out.

If you need a script to get you started, try saying the following when your brain feels pregnant with fear: "Jesus, I bind up these thoughts of fear and cast them into the pit of hell in Jesus' name. I am a daughter of the King, and no weapon formed against me shall prosper! I am a daughter of the King!"

Speaking these words out loud might feel funny at first, but they will bring forth the authority that God has given you because words have power. It will also encourage you more than you could ever imagine. Speak with the authority that you've been given, and confront those fears with God's truth.

3. Put It In Writing

Finally, when confronting your fears, the art of journaling will be a powerful tool for you. It's important to get very clear on what bravery and courage look like in your own life. Think of the movies that you've watched where bravery and courage have been displayed. What was it about the characters that you identified with? Write out a clear picture of the qualities and habits a brave and courageous person has so you can begin to ask God for wisdom in how to emulate them in your own life. The Personal Reflection questions at the end of this chapter will help you with this as well.

A crazy, awesome, and supernatural thing happens when we put pen to paper. Be brave enough to confront your fears by writing out your own path of courage.

•••

As we close this chapter, remember this powerful truth: a child of God has absolutely nothing to fear. There's no lie, label, or fear that can shackle you when you embrace this truth. You no longer have to walk around with those nasty lies and labels written on your heart. No. You are a brave woman! Choose to rise up, out of the ashes of fear, and embrace the courage that is rightfully yours. It's already in you! Apply the tools that have been outlined for you in this chapter, and walk with your head held high as the overcomer that you are.

TRUTH ABOUT ME STATEMENTS:

- I have no fear of bad news. My heart is steadfast, and I trust in the Lord.
- I am not the labels that other people have put on me or that I have put on myself. I am courageous and fearless!
- I have authority to overcome the power of the enemy, as well as the lies, labels, and fears that have been stopping me.
- I am a courageous overcomer.
- When I am weak, He is strong!

PERSONAL REFLECTION TIME:

- What are the lies and labels that others have put on you, or that you have put on yourself?
- Would you say you are more afraid of success or of failure? Why?
- How would you describe a fearless woman?
- Think of a situation that you are currently afraid of. How can you display courage in that this week?
- What has God been telling you as you confront your lies, labels, and fears?

RELATED WORDS OF LIFE TO STUDY:

"She will have no fear of bad news; her heart is steadfast, trusting in the Lord. Her heart is secure, she will have no fear; in the end she will look in triumph on her foes." ~Psalm 112:7-8

"I have given you authority to trample on snakes and scorpions and to overcome all the power of the enemy; nothing will harm you." ~Luke 10:19

"But he said to me, 'My grace is sufficient for you, for my power is made perfect in weakness.' Therefore I will boast all the more gladly about my weaknesses, so that Christ's power may rest on me. That is why, for Christ's sake, I delight in weaknesses, in insults, in hardships, in persecutions, in difficulties. For when I am weak, then I am strong." ~2 Corinthians 12:9-10, NIV

"Even though I walk through the darkest valley, I will fear no evil, for you are with me; your rod and your staff, they comfort me." ~Psalm 23:4, NIV

"For I am the Lord your God who takes hold of your right hand and says to you, Do not fear; I will help you." ~Isaiah 41:13, NIV

"Moses answered the people, "Do not be afraid. Stand firm and you will see the deliverance the Lord will bring you today." ~Exodus 14:13, NIV

"Be strong and courageous. Do not be afraid or terrified because of them, for the Lord your God goes with you; he

will never leave you nor forsake you." ~Deuteronomy 31:6, NIV

"For the Spirit God gave us does not make us timid, but gives us power, love and self-discipline." ~2 Timothy 1:7, NIV

"The Lord is my light and my salvation—whom shall I fear? The Lord is the stronghold of my life—of whom shall I be afraid?" ~Psalm 27:1, NIV

"So we say with confidence, "The Lord is my helper; I will not be afraid. What can mere mortals do to me?" ~Hebrews 13:6, NIV

"Peace I leave with you; my peace I give you. I do not give to you as the world gives. Do not let your hearts be troubled and do not be afraid." ~John 14:27, NIV

8

She is Brave Enough to Keep Going

~courage to look crazy~

~ JOURNAL ENTRY ~

May 3, 2012

Dear Lord,

Well...I've been in the hospital for four days now. Back to doing treatments and on tons of antibiotics. This morning my doctor didn't have any good news. In fact, my entire medical team looks at me with tears in their eyes and can't seem to find the words to say, which basically makes the situation seem quite dire. But I DO see good news. For instance, my oxygen levels are coming back up. I showered by myself today. I've gained 3 pounds since being admitted. My lungs sound clear. I have peace that I'm doing the right thing by being here...

But Lord, when I have too much time to think my mind wanders. And the places it travels to don't offer a lot of hope. And I haven't actually spent time with you because I'm tired, lonely, and I feel like you've abandoned me. But you promise that you'll never leave me nor forsake me so I know that you're here. Lord, heal my hurting heart. It is so wounded right now...in many ways. And heal my body...forgive me if I've been wrong the last two years. I still believe you've healed me in some way and that I will recover from all of this. But I really need You right now.

●●●

Overcomers are not bullet proof. We feel pain and sorrow and sometimes...sometimes we get weary. Sometimes we feel abandoned. Sometimes we need encouragement. Sometimes we need a sign that we're on the right path.

That's where Revelation 3:8-11 comes in.

"I see what you've done. Now see what I've done. I've opened a door before you that no one can slam shut. You don't have much strength, I know that; you used what you had to keep my Word. You didn't deny me when times were rough.

And watch as I take those who call themselves true believers but are nothing of the kind, pretenders whose true membership is in the club of Satan – watch as I strip off their pretensions and they're forced to acknowledge it's you that I've loved.

Because you kept my Word in passionate patience, I'll keep you safe in the time of testing that will be here soon, and all over the earth, every man, woman, and child put to the test.

I'm on my way; I'll be there soon. Keep a tight grip on what you have so no one distracts you and steals your crown."
~Revelation 3:8-11, *MSG*

My eyes have read over these words countless times, when my soul was desperate for encouragement. When I was unsure about taking a leap of faith, these words reassured me. When I was struggling to find meaning in the valley of loss, these words helped me to keep going. And when I felt like a failure, these words helped shift my perspective.

"Now see what I've done."

In verse eight, God is literally asking us to view our circumstances in a different light. When we're tired and weary and have lost all of our strength, it's easy to be a downer. It's easy to be negative and crabby. It's easy to feel hopeless. Yet, it is in those moments that God wraps His arms around us and reminds us to take another peek. Walk away from our agendas, our broken hearts, and our weary feelings so we can look at things from His perspective. Even in our darkest moments, He has opened a door that only He can open.

I'm encouraged not only by the reminder that God is keeping me safe, but also by the characteristics that He celebrates in this passage. He reminds his people of the ways that they have overcome:

- They held on even when they were weary.
- They didn't deny Jesus when times got rough.
- They activated patience and endured.
- They were steadfast.
- They didn't get distracted by pettiness but instead held on to God's promises and visions.
- They looked to God and for God in every situation.

They held on to their faith and kept going, even when others thought they were crazy. That's what overcomers do. Even when they are weary, they keep going. Even when they are caught up in pain and sorrow, they keep going. Even when they feel abandoned, they keep going. Yes, they might need to have some encouragement. They might need to be refilled with truth and love. But no matter what, overcomers stay focused on the doors that God is opening, and they willingly keep going forward without looking back on the doors that God has closed. They are never afraid to keep going.

~ BRAVE ENOUGH TO WALK FORWARD ~

Vulnerable. Heart cracked wide open for you to see. That's how I feel as I begin to bring this chapter together for you. From the very beginning of this project, I knew that this would be the hardest chapter to write because it's the most personal. Yet, I have this...feeling that...maybe you can identify with my journal entry from a moment ago. Maybe there's been a time in your life where the places that your mind wandered to didn't offer much hope. Maybe you've experienced seasons where you've felt tired, lonely, and abandoned by God, too. Maybe the ashes in your life have been choking you and burying you so deep that you feel as though the end is right around the corner. Maybe you really need Him right now, in this very moment. It's because of that very real possibility that I feel a moral obligation to share a very personal story with you that paints a picture of what Revelation 3:8-11 looks like in real life, even though I feel slightly afraid of it. So here goes.

There was a time in my life where all I wanted was to experience a supernatural, full physical healing of cystic fibrosis. I believe that God heals diseases even when there is no cure available. I've met people who have been paralyzed with no hopes of medical intervention, and they now walk because God healed them. I believe this happens, and I wanted to experience it myself. I wanted to be done with the treatments and free of the bondage. I wanted to walk away from it all and have documentation that proved God's work in my life. I wanted to know what it was like to be normal, without the haunting ghost named cystic fibrosis forever following me around. This desire became so strong that it was my prayer for several years; I sought this with everything in me. As I did, the journey God led me on became one that taught me bravery, faith, and the depth of God's love like I had never known before.

If you would have told me in my teenage years that there would be a two-year season in my life where I stopped doing the breathing treatments and medication required to survive from CF, I would have thought you were crazy. My parents raised me to be responsible. They also raised me to walk by faith. Sometimes the two don't look anything alike.

In March of 2010, at a business event in Jacksonville, Florida, I felt God Almighty touch my body in a way I had never experienced before. As my business coach prayed for a physical healing of CF over me, I felt a stirring in the depths of my soul, and my lungs began to drain in a funny way. Oh, I had been to plenty of "healing services" in the past, and I'd always come away from them completely hopeful and excited only to find that my lung functions had dropped over the last few months instead of getting better, even though I had done all of my medication faithfully and remained the model patient. This time was different. This time I felt amazing. I went back to my hotel room that evening and told God that I was "all in!" There was no going back – I was one-hundred percent committed to walking by faith, and so I took all my medication and flushed it down the toilet. (Please hear me loud and clear – I am not giving any medical advice here! I am simply telling you the facts of what happened to me personally.)

The next morning I woke up, breathing better than ever before, and I did something I could never do – I ran a mile with absolutely no pain and no gasping for air! It was amazing! A week later I was still running, only now I was also singing while I ran on the treadmill! Nate just stood there and stared at me with a big smile on his face. The fact that I could run, and had so much energy, built my faith because this should have been impossible given the fact that I had not done any breathing treatments or asthma inhalers for days.

As time went on, and people around me expressed fear and doubt of God's ability to heal CF, the spiritual warfare became thick. The medical documentation I had hoped to see didn't quite add up, and I began to learn the valuable lesson of believing God's promises instead of the medical reports. My lung functions dropped from about eighty-five percent of normal down to seventy-five percent and then to fifty percent eight months after that night in March. You might be thinking to yourself, "Gosh Mandy, how stupid are you?!" Believe me, I wondered at times too but I must confess – I felt so good, so strong, and I could RUN for twenty minutes at a time and never once felt pain like I did before when I tried to run down the block. I even ran my first ever 5K race during this time. That's something I never imagined I could accomplish!

~ YOUR CRAZY IS SHOWING ~

Bold faith often looks crazy to those who are not on the same path. Throwing my medication away and choosing to walk by faith that God would heal my body with His touch alone, was one of the craziest things I've ever done. But I felt deep in my heart that this was the path I was to take. I just didn't know why at the time.

The months turned into years, and after a devastating miscarriage in December of 2011, along with the remaining stress of PTSD from the fire, it became harder and harder to hold on to my faith and believe that I truly was healed of CF. Buried emotions and deep trauma can make the human body physically ill, and the symptoms closely mirrored those of this disease. Panic attacks made my chest hurt, coughing attacks began happening every morning, and I constantly questioned whether it was CF or the deep depression and sadness I found myself in that was causing the pain. Truthfully, it was probably a little bit of both, the perfect storm just waiting for the perfect moment to unleash its wrath.

There were nights where Nate and I would wake up and pray for hours because I would have a coughing attack that came out of nowhere. As soon as we got done praying, the coughing would be gone, and it would stay away for a few days. When people around me became skeptical of God's ability to heal CF, my body would react to it by coughing the entire time we were together. But then I would spend time with my closest friends who would encourage me and pray for me, and you wouldn't hear me cough once. It was so strange…and quite frustrating to be honest.

In the moments where I began to feel as crazy as people were beginning to think I was, I would look for the proof: I could run. With no pain. I could sing. Even at fifty percent lung functions, which one respiratory therapist told me, after hearing me sing at a conference, should be impossible to do. It was the craziest season of life that I had ever walked through.

~ IF THESE WALLS COULD TALK ~

The pages of my journals from the five months of January to May 2012 are marked with the persistent, courageous, desperate, and vulnerable cries of a wounded soldier in spiritual warfare. If the yellow walls of our apartment during that season could talk, they would paint a frightening picture.

On the weeks when Nate was gone for work, loneliness would swallow me whole. Hours would pass before I'd find the strength to get out of bed. Several times I spent more than thirty minutes in the shower, hunched over on the floor hugging my legs as my tears mixed in with searing hot water, drifting down the drain in search of a happier dwelling place. Standing up was becoming more of a chore than I ever realized it could be as my legs were becoming weaker by the day, all of my energy used up to supply the simple task of breathing that had become not so simple after all. Every muscle in my body ached, and even the idea of hugging another person painted a picture of such physical pain that I walked around hunched over, hugging myself protectively to keep others from adding to the torture. Cracked ribs and chest pains were my new normal, and daily morning panic attacks made me drop five pounds nearly each week. I saw myself wasting away every time I looked in the mirror. My emaciated frame was not the picture of health and healing that I imagined. It hurt to look at myself, and the lies and labels of skinny sick girl screamed louder than they ever had before.

Not knowing where to turn for comfort, I often found myself doing the only thing I could think to do – reading the Bible. God's words were the only thing that soothed my broken spirit. There were nights where the coughing attacks were so treacherous that all I could do was cry out to God for healing and scream out His promises. Sometimes the screams were more questions of "Where are you?!" than confessions of faith. Other times I could barely get a whisper out, and my prayers were nothing more than lips moving without sound. Faith seemed to be all that I had left, and it was hanging by a thread. Everything I thought my life would be was crumbling at my feet, yet somewhere deep inside me I knew that God's promises would show themselves true in due time. If only I could hang on long enough to see them come to pass.

The situation looked hopeless. It looked as though the end was near and happiness was forever lost to the living hell that I found myself fighting to get out of. Yet, even in the darkest moments, God's words rang loud and clear. One night I felt a love letter being written across my heart, and I penned it in the pages of my journal…

>   *My child,*
>   *We will work through this together. I will not abandon you nor will I destroy you…this will not destroy you. Just as a seed has to die before it sprouts, you are dying to old destructive thought patterns and being molded by truth. You have bondage breaking faith, boldness, and courage to face painful things for my glory. I gave you that boldness. I gave you that courage…I gave you that faith. For a long time it has been trampled on but it is better to trust in the Lord than to trust in man – even if that means trusting God over your loved ones. This is the time to trust me fully. Seek me with all of your heart and all your mind and all your soul and you will find me. My promises are true. I will never leave you nor forsake you. I will not make you feel guilty or manipulate you or try to control*

you. I will listen to you, love you, console you, renew you, and guide you. I will carry you through this. I am the Lord Almighty – is anything too hard for Me?

I didn't realize it at the time, but I do now. This letter was not just for me; it was for you, too.

If the walls of that apartment could talk, they would tell you that in the deepest, darkest moments of my life, I cried out to God, and He showed up. It might not have happened in the way that I had planned it to, but it happened. He rescued me. He carried me. He restored me. And He will do the same for you, my friend, no matter what circumstance you find yourself in right now.

•••

On the morning of April 30, 2012, Nate wheeled me into the clinic. I had no strength to walk; I barely had enough strength to breathe. I weighed ninety-three pounds fully clothed and my lung functions had dropped down to twenty-two percent. I was admitted into the hospital and put on oxygen right away. This was the first time I had ever needed oxygen. The entire CF team, who had known me to be a very compliant patient, was in tears. They were relieved that I finally came into the hospital, but I could see the fear in their eyes.

I spent the next twenty-two days in the hospital.

I was too weak to even bathe myself during those first few days, so Nate had to live out his "in sickness and in health" vows by helping me shower and wash my hair. I have never loved him more than I did in those very vulnerable, precious moments. His love was so strong, so full of faith when he had every right to be weak.

In the quiet moments of those first few days in that stark, dreary hospital room, I often wondered to myself if I did something wrong. Was I not faithful enough? Was I really crazy to think God would heal me completely of cystic fibrosis? No one can deny that

I experienced some divine health over those two years. My doctor had even admitted several months prior to this hospitalization that things didn't make sense. At the time I wasn't sure why God was allowing me to experience such pain and heartache, such...doubt. I didn't understand back then why I was fighting for my life, the door of death so close, instead of enjoying the ease of life with a physical healing. None of it made any sense to me. All I could do was hold on to His promises and trust that God knew what was best. He always knows what is best.

The third night that I was in the hospital, I somehow found the strength to stand up on my own and look in the mirror. The face I found there was one that took my breath away in a moment of horror and desperation; I didn't even recognize the woman staring back at me. Oxygen tubes lined my gaunt, bony cheeks. My skin looked gray, the luster long gone. But worst of all, my eyes looked...lost. The spark of happiness and life that was once there had been replaced with the hollow residue of depression, sickness, and hopelessness.

It is by the grace of God that, in that moment, I realized I had a choice. I could be bitter about the cards I had been dealt with in life and continue focusing on how much I felt God let me down, or I could choose to be thankful for my life and the time that was left. I looked at myself in the mirror and said, "Mandy, this will not be the end of your story. God has promised you that He will rescue you and carry you even to your old age and gray hair! This is not the end. Fight. Fight for the life God has given you."

To be honest, I wasn't sure how things would unfold exactly. It was a very real possibility that a life of physical limitations, sickness, and struggle would be my new normal. All I did know was that it was time to be thankful for the medicine and thankful for the time I now had in the hospital to rest and recharge. God would work out the rest of my confused, hurt feelings in His timing.

His timing turned out to be a little sooner than I had anticipated. Two days later, my friend Madison stopped by my hospital room with the biggest salad she could find. My appetite had been lacking for months now and I was supposed to be eating anything and everything so I could gain weight, yet all I wanted was a salad. So she delivered as only a best friend can. She handed me the container and then took a seat on the bed, her true intentions for the visit about to be revealed.

"Mandy, I have something to tell you," she began to speak as tears of compassion and love filled her eyes. "I feel like God wants you to know that it's okay. You don't have to hold on to this idea of healing without medicine anymore. No one thinks you're weak. You haven't let God down. He is not mad at you, nor is He punishing you. You haven't let anyone else down at all. We just want you to get better so you can live those dreams you've talked about so much. I give you permission to let go and let God work through medicine."

Tears began to overflow as my heart began to receive the words that she had just spoken over me. Her precious words were an answer to my prayers.

Maybe you need the kind of permission that Madison gave to me. Maybe you need to let go and let God work in ways that are different than you had imagined when you first began the journey that you find yourself on. Can I be honest with you? It takes more courage to hold on to your faith and look crazy than to give up on God altogether because things didn't work out like you thought it would.

So I give you permission today, to let go and let God. Let God work in your life. Muster up the courage to trust Him, keep holding on to your faith, even when things don't look like you dreamed they would.

~ WHEN THE HEALING DOESN'T COME ~

"Now see what I've done."

Those words from Revelation should never be forgotten or ignored.

In the nearly three years since that experience, I have come to realize that the real healing that needed to take place wasn't in my body – it was in my heart. He knew that the thing I was really yearning for with everything in me was a healing and a freedom from the fear and burden of what CF could become. And that's what He healed. The fear, the worry, the burden, the wondering if God will take care of me – all of that is gone. It's all completely washed away. Because I now know - with everything in me - that God will rescue me from my sickbed and restore me from my bed of illness.

He allowed me to experience all of my worst fears, and then He rescued me and restored my joy and my health. I now fully understand what it's like to suffer with this disease. I get how debilitating it is to have to crawl down the hallway gasping for air because that's actually easier than trying to walk down the hallway. I've faced CF related diabetes head on and learned how to check my own blood sugars and give myself insulin. I've discussed the option of a feeding tube, and even though I shed some tears over the truth that those setbacks might become my reality, I overcame them and thanked God for a second chance at life.

He allowed me to face my worst fears and experience such horrible things so that I could get to this place; so that this story could get to you. He knows how badly you needed to hear this story. He brought you here; I didn't.

When the healing doesn't come the way we want, when the situation takes a drastic turn for the worst, when we feel weary and want to give up, we must choose to activate those words in Revelation, *"Now see what I've done."*

If we don't direct our thoughts, they will always be the enemy of our spirit, of our faith. We can know something in our spirit, we can have faith that God's words are true and will prevail, but our thoughts will tell us that it is not right. They will scream at us, *"You're crazy!"* Sometimes our thoughts and our emotions will even partner together, making us feel completely hopeless! We must learn to seek God in everything. Seek Him when your thoughts say, *"I'm never going to get better."* Seek Him when your emotions are full of fear. Seek Him when the doctors can't figure out what's going on in your body. Keep seeking Him when you feel like giving up because your spirit knows the truth. Your spirit knows that every single promise in the Bible is for YOU. Your spirit knows this and is waiting for you to activate your faith. Encourage yourself in that!

"Now see what I've done."

When I pause to see what God has done through my hopeless looking circumstances, here is what I find:

Several of the professionals on my medical team have told me that they doubted that I would ever see lung functions above forty percent. The damage to my lungs after two years without treatments was bound to be severe. They also told me to be prepared to be a diabetic for the rest of my life. I'm so excited to report that today my lung functions are at seventy-six percent and climbing, my weight is stable, I never needed that feeding tube, and I no longer have to take insulin. That, my friends, is the work of a gracious God. Yes, He is using medicine as His method to heal my body, but all glory goes to Him and Him alone!

My friend, if you are yearning for a healing in your body or your life, I encourage you to keep asking God. Keep seeking Him. Study His word on healing and ask Him to give you wisdom. I'm here to tell you that God does heal. Sometimes He gives divine, physical healing. Sometimes He uses medicine to restore your health. Sometimes the healing happens in our emotions and our hearts. I don't know why it happens in different ways. All I know is that His promises are true, and He will always fight for us and provide for us.

~ FINDING THE COURAGE TO LOOK CRAZY ~

"I see what you've done. Now see what I've done. I've opened a door before you that no one can slam shut. You don't have

much strength, I know that; you used what you had to keep my Word. You didn't deny me when times were rough." ~Revelation 3:8-11, *MSG*

It might not seem like it at first glance, but this verse is all about faith. Read it again and you'll see it. It's about hanging on to God when your strength is gone and your faith feels fragile. That's the visual definition of faith! Faith is being sure of what we hope for and confident of what we don't see (Hebrews 11:1). And faith is never more important than in those moments when all of the evidence counteracts our faith. When we hold on to our faith in the direst of circumstances, God doesn't ignore it. He rewards it. He opens new doors in the midst of it and extends a hand for us to walk through it with Him. We must be diligent in looking for what He is doing when our faith is weak and the evidence is against us.

I've come to discover that the easiest part of faith is the first step. The first step is filled with excitement and blind trust in God. It's easy to get excited and pumped up when you're in the moment; it's the steps that follow that make it hard. Those are the steps that wind through the tunnels of second-guessing, questioning, comparison, and worry. We don't need proof for the first step because we see the door that God has opened for us. But when we walk over the threshold, we often find that this new room isn't a room at all – it's a hallway.

When you find yourself in that hallway, be brave enough to keep going. Find the courage, even if you look crazy to everyone around you. Don't give up or run to your comfort zone. Embrace the strength that the overcomers displayed in Revelation 3:8-11.

- Hold on when you feel weary.
- Endure.
- Activate patience.
- Remain steadfast.
- Hold on to God's promises and do not deny Jesus.
- Look to God, and for God, in every situation.

- Use the strength that you do have to hold on to God's Word!

Activate bondage-breaking faith. It is a faith that breaks the bondage of disease, doubt, and worry. It may or may not mean that you still have an ailment; however, it always means that in the midst of it all, with bondage-breaking faith, God will heal your heart so you can fully trust Him with your life! What does it matter if you live your whole life with an illness that requires treatments and occasional hospital visits? When God is with you – opening doors that NO MAN can shut – our circumstances don't matter. What matters is that He is there. He is working in you and through you. That's what matters. That's all that matters.

•••

Dear Jesus,

Thank you for reminding me that you are keeping me safe, and you are always here for me. Forgive me for not always looking to you when I'm weary. Forgive me for seeking comfort in others instead of your Word and your comforting arms. Forgive me for ignoring you in the moments when my faith feels weak and my heart is hurt. Help me to see things from your perspective. Help me to celebrate the characteristics of an overcomer that you have put in me, and to go after the doors that you're opening. Jesus, I don't want to be stuck in the past any more. I don't want to be stuck in sadness or disappointment any longer. I'm ready to say goodbye to the doors that You've closed so I can fully embrace the new things that You're doing in my life.

In Jesus' name, Amen

TRUTH ABOUT ME STATEMENTS:

- I am a woman of bondage-breaking faith.
- I am brave enough to keep going, even when I'm weary, even when I feel as though others think I'm crazy.
- I will hold on to God's truth in every situation.
- I will look to God, and for God, in every situation.
- I will use the strength that I do have to hold on when I am weary.

PERSONAL REFLECTION TIME:

- When you read Revelation 3:8-11, what jumps out at you the most?
- How do you identify with my story of faith and healing?
- What doors has God opened for you that you need to walk through by faith?
- What doors has God closed for you that you need to release fully to Him and stop looking back on?
- What characteristics from this passage do you already have in you?
- What is God saying to you right now, in this moment?

RELATED WORDS OF LIFE TO STUDY:

"May the God of hope fill you with all joy and peace as you trust in him, so that you may overflow with hope by the power of the Holy Spirit." ~Romans 15:13, NIV

"So let God work his will in you. Yell a loud no to the Devil and watch him scamper. Say a quiet yes to God and he'll

be there in no time. Quit dabbling in sin. Purify your inner life. Quit playing the field. Hit bottom, and cry your eyes out. The fun and games are over. Get serious, really serious. Get down on your knees before your Master; it's the only way you'll get on your feet." ~James 4:7-10, MSG

"Forget the former things; do not dwell on the past. See, I am doing a new thing! Now it springs up; do you not perceive it? I am making a way in the desert and streams in the wasteland." ~Isaiah 43:18-19, NIV

"Now faith is confidence in what we hope for and assurance about what we do not see." ~Hebrews 11:1, NLT

~ section III ~

REDEMPTION

MANDY B. ANDERSON

9

She Remembers Her First Love

~redeemed of past mistakes~

My ears popped, and I sat with my head against the headrest as the plane rose higher and higher in the sky. It was only three days after our apartment fire, and I found myself going through the motions of flying to a business conference in Orlando, Florida. I almost didn't go, but some close friends encouraged me to get away for a while and try to enjoy myself. Apparently I looked like I needed a break from the stress of my new reality.

As the plane gained altitude, we flew over the ashes of the apartment building. I put my forehead against the cold window and felt a tear trickle down my cheek. It looked so small from thirteen thousand feet above the ground. I wondered how such a small building that disappeared when I placed my thumb on the window could be the burial place of all of my belongings and cherished keepsakes. In the quiet of that moment, I heard some words dance across my heart over and over again. They kept repeating themselves in a melody, and I could hear a haunting piano tune swirling around them.

I took out my pen and wrote the following words of a song...

When the flames devour everything and all I have is vanishing,
Lord, you are enough.
When the pain is welling up and faith is all I've got,
Lord, you are enough.

You can strip me of all I have.
You can break me and put me back together again.
In my weakness I know you're here.
And Lord, you will always be...
Enough.

By the time the plane landed in Orlando, I could hear the entire song. I had not played piano for a few months, but I had this sense of urgency that I needed to find one. As it turned out, the conference center I had arrived at just happened to have a baby grand piano hiding in a secluded hallway. I sat down on the piano bench, placed my fingers on the black and white keys, and let the emotional weights fall of off me in the form of a brand new tune. It was a very healing moment.

•••

Overcomers know, in their darkest moments, that if they have God, then they have all that they need. They know that His love, His provision, His redemption...they are all enough. Yet, even with this deep knowledge, sometimes we must be reminded of what the heartbeat of our soul really is.

We began our journey together in Revelation 2:7-11. You may have noticed by now that we skipped a letter at the beginning of Revelation, Chapter Two. The reason is simple and strategic. Journeying through what it takes to persist and embrace courage is often easier than learning how to embrace God's love and redemption. But learning to embrace His love and redemption is just as important, if not more, so let's rewind our study for a moment and let God's words cover our hearts again with some important reminders and warnings.

"I see what you've done, your hard, hard work, your refusal to quit. I know you can't stomach evil, that you weed out apostolic pretenders. I know your persistence, your courage in my cause, that you never wear out.

But you walked away from your first love—why? What's going on with you, anyway? Do you have any idea how far you've fallen? A Lucifer fall!

Turn back! Recover your dear early love. No time to waste, for I'm well on my way to removing your light from the golden circle.

You do have this to your credit: You hate the Nicolaitan business. I hate it, too.

Are your ears awake? Listen. Listen to the Wind Words, the Spirit blowing through the churches. I'm about to call each conqueror to dinner. I'm spreading a banquet of Tree-of-Life fruit, a supper plucked from God's orchard." ~Revelation 2:2-7, MSG

The life of an overcomer is marked with the traces of extreme persistence and courage. God values that, as He states in these verses. We've spent two-thirds of our time together uncovering what that looks like, acts like, and speaks like in many different situations. Before we end our journey together, we've got to uncover one more important quality that all overcomers must embrace. It's something that comes only from Jesus Christ: redemption.

Overcomers are not supposed to be do-it-yourselfers. In fact, one of the most important qualities that overcomers display is the ability to admit that they don't have it all figured out, that they need God and others to help them along the way. The words that define the essence of redemption include words like salvation, deliverance, atonement, and restitution. That's what Jesus has for all who overcome and trust in Him. And sometimes overcomers must humble themselves and just admit that they need God to rescue them.

But there's more…

The words of Revelation 2:7 tell us that one of the rewards of being an overcomer is that we get to eat from the tree of life again. Let's rewind for a moment to the very beginning of time. When Adam was first placed in the garden, he had this right. Eve had this right. They were both able to eat from the tree of life, but after they chose to sin, this right was taken away. (See Genesis 2:9-3:22 for the whole sad story.) The beautiful thing about God is that He redeems our mistakes. He restores us, even when we've messed up. If you read it carefully, you'll discover that restoration happens when we overcome!

How excited God must be when we become overcomers through His son Jesus Christ! When we choose Him! That's the reward – a restored invite to God's banquet table. So how do we get there? In this letter to the Church in Ephesus, we see that the people of this church have done a few things well, but they've also lost sight of one very important detail. First, here's what they did right:

1. They overcame laziness and an attitude of giving up. They were persistent and courageous. (Rev. 2:2)
2. They also overcame evil. They didn't tolerate wicked people or false prophets. (Rev. 2:2)

But then they dropped the ball. In verse four we see that they not only forgot their first love, they abandoned Him. After spending time devouring the first two sections of this book, we now know without a doubt that becoming an overcomer requires persistence. It demands hard work and courage. We've seen this and devoured it over the last eight chapters. It also begs us to stand boldly for truth – especially when it's against those who do evil. These are all noble qualities. Great qualities. There's nothing wrong them. But those qualities alone don't determine whether we will overcome by God's standards. In fact, the words from this passage that bring shivers to my spine, are those from verse four...

"Yet I hold this against you: You have forsaken your first love. Remember the height from which you have fallen! Repent and do the things you did at first."

That one hurts a bit. It forces me to stop and take inventory of my motives; it begs me to check my heart.

~ FALLING IN LOVE ~

The other day on social media, I asked our friends to describe their first love in one word. Some of the words used were husband and mom, identifying the source of this first human love. Others used words such as exciting, patient, intoxicating, forever, sweet, wonderful, educating, and even heartbreaking. These words all described the experience of that first human love that we carry with us forever.

My first real love, the one that made the biggest impact on my life, was not my first boyfriend, but rather a boy that I had known almost my entire life. In first grade, he made his friends hold me down on the playground while he planted a big kiss on my lips. Of course, I didn't appreciate that one bit and vowed that I would never ever ever never in a million years like this boy, let alone date him. Never. Ever. (Sigh) And then I found myself falling for him head over heels during our senior year of high school. It was thrilling, intoxicating, and in the end, heartbreaking. It didn't end in the fairy tale way that I had dreamed it would at the tender age of eighteen. The choices that were made on both sides of that relationship resulted in deep pain for each of us. I spent years in denial of how I had really felt in that relationship and about the whole experience overall, and only recently has God opened the door to complete healing in my heart. Not all first love experiences are colored with sunshine and rainbows and happily ever afters.

Falling in love with my husband was different. The start of our romance is best colored in words like exciting, patient, forgiving, and forever. It was full of all of those wonderful, exciting, and breathtaking moments that falling in love encompasses. When my husband and I first started dating over a decade ago, we couldn't wait to spend time together. We would often fall asleep on the phone talking to each other because we didn't want to hang up. We would walk and talk for hours, fingers entwined, dreaming about the future. We couldn't get enough of each other! Somehow I knew, even in those first initial months, that he would be in my life forever. Obviously, we said, "I do." And even through the years of hardships, chaos, and pain, our love has endured. We have proven that not all love ends in heartbreak.

•••

When I read the words, "Remember your first love," in Revelation Chapter Two, and I recall that the lover of my soul is Jesus Christ, I have to stop and think: Do I treat Jesus like I did when I first met Him? Have I ever treated Him with the adoration that I gave my husband during those first love years? Do I yearn to spend time with Jesus more than with anyone or anything else?

I hate to admit it, but my answer to those questions is often no. Sometimes I avoid spending time with Him because it's less emotionally exhausting to tune out in front of my favorite television show. Many mornings I race through our time together because I overslept, and my earthly responsibilities are beckoning me. It's as though I am rushing out the door yelling, "Sorry, Jesus! Not today. I love You, though, I really do! Thank You for always being there for me! I'll catch You later when I've got nothing better to do!"

Ouch. Not my best moments. And according to this scripture, if I'm courageous, hard working, stand for truth, and never give up – until I repent for forgetting and abandoning my first love, I'm not really an overcomer. That doesn't sit well with me. Chances are, as you reach a similar realization, it's not sitting well with you either.

Think about it for a moment. When was the last time you really spent quality time with the lover of your soul? When you first met Jesus, how did He capture your heart? What music brought you closer to Him? How did He make you feel? The process of reminiscing about our love for Jesus is the same as reminiscing about the first days of love with our spouse. Answering those questions, and taking the time to stroll down memory lane, reminds us of why we fell in love, and how much we have grown and overcome together since then. It's an important process, not just for a marriage, but for remembering the one true lover of our souls – Jesus Christ – as well.

If I'm honest with you, this is an area that I'm still growing in. I don't have it all figured out, and my understanding of this process is still so small. Yet, I've been called to share it with you because of its importance in the journey that all overcomers must take. However, what I can tell you is what it looks like when you've forgotten your first love, and how that affects every area of your life.

You see, in my experience, the years where I forgot my first love the most, were the years where I was bored and unhappy. Nate and I lived more like roommates than spouses because somehow we had forgotten how to show our love to each other. It's quite ironic to me now that my marriage reflected the spiritual health of my heart because the more I neglected to show love to Nate, the further I got from showing love to God and receiving his love for me. My identity was confused at best and messed up at worst.

I tried filling that emptiness and longing with watching television, performing better, and even flirting with other guys even though I was married. I'm not proud of those years – they almost cost me my marriage and so much more. But I am thankful for them. They taught me how to recognize when I am neglecting my marriage as well as my first love – Jesus.

~ WARNING SIGNS OF FORGETTING YOUR FIRST LOVE ~

Right now you're probably thinking to yourself, "Mandy, this all makes sense, but how exactly do you know if you've forgotten your first love?" Well, I'm so glad you asked! When we spend time with the people whom we love, we often become like them. We begin to say the same things and even adopt similar thought patterns. It's the same when we spend time with Jesus. There are many character traits and behaviors that give us clues that our heart is off track and our relationship with him is waning. Let's take a look at several of them.

1. Comparisons and Low Self-Esteem.

Anytime we begin to compare ourselves to others and our self-esteem feels depleted, we have begun the process of forgetting our first love. Our approval should only come from Jesus, and when we look to others to find it, our relationship with Him is in dire need of rescue.

2. Discontentment and Boredom.

When we abide in the love of Jesus, life is anything but boring. He is the source of happiness and joy! When we begin to feel discontented, unhappy as can be, and bored out of our minds, chances are we have lost track of our relationship with Him.

3. Unforgiveness and Holding Grudges.

Jesus is the very essence of forgiveness. His redemption is offered to us through forgiveness and grace. When we hold grudges against others and refuse to forgive them for the hurts they've caused us, we are neglecting our first love. We must embrace our first love again, ask Him to forgive us, and forgive ourselves and others as well.

4. Being Easily Offended.

When our focus is on the opinions of others, it is no longer on Jesus. Offense happens when we worry more about what others think of us than what Jesus thinks and says about us.

5. Lack of Spiritual Food (i.e., God's word).

When we refuse to read God's word, and our Bible's collect dust or our Bible app hasn't been opened in months, we are spiritually starved. God's word is the love letter that our soul desperately longs for! When we refuse to open it, it's as though we have sent His letters back stamped with the words, "Return to sender." How heartbreaking that must be for the lover of our soul!

6. Excessive Loneliness.

When we feel lonely, we have chosen to look at our circumstances through the wrong lens. Loneliness is an invitation to spend more time with Jesus. When we refuse to do so, that loneliness eats us up inside.

7. Self-centeredness.

When we make everything all about us, we take our eyes off of Jesus. Plain and simple. The more we focus on our wants, our let downs, our sadness, our pain, the less we can see his love for us. Think about it. Do you enjoy spending time with someone who always makes the conversation about them? It's the same with Jesus. When we are self-centered, we have forgotten our first love and we need to return to Him so our pride can be diminished.

8. Speaking Negatively About Yourself and Others.

When we abide in the love of Jesus, His fruit naturally comes out of us. We begin to love others and learn how to edify and uplift them with our words. We also learn how to encourage ourselves and build ourselves up with our own words. A negative, gossiping tongue is one that has forgotten its first love.

9. Being Judgmental.

Love doesn't judge others. If we spend all of our time judging the way another person acts, speaks, and looks, then we are not spending enough time with Jesus. Period.

~ REDEEMED OF PAST MISTAKES ~

The love of Jesus is a powerful love that redeems us of so many things, including our past mistakes. As we remember our first love, and return to Him, He washes us clean. Our mistakes no longer hold us captive; instead they serve as a tool that helps shape us for God's glory.

Getting back on track is often easier than we make it out to be. If you identified with the warning signs of forgetting your first love, and you are ready to get back on track, here are some simple action steps to take:

1. Repent by asking Him to forgive you today.
2. Receive His forgiveness and let Him redeem your mistakes and make a vow to get back on track.
3. Spend time in God's word and journal the conversations that you have with Him. Listen quietly for His voice.
4. Listen to podcast sermons or worship music that encourages you.

A true overcomer pays attention to the warning signs and always remembers her first love. It's not your high school kind of first love that risks creating heartache and pain most likely to be stuffed away in baggage and carried around for years to come. No. His love is different. It's a forever kind of love that mends, and heals, and stretches, and reaches those deepest places in your heart like no other love can.

Do you know this love? Have you ever known this love? If you have, you'll feel the ache of it when you neglect it. If you listen closely, Jesus is speaking to your heart right now, begging you to return to Him, or possibly come to Him for the first time ever. Dear friend, won't you answer His invitation? Remember your first love, your heart's one true desire. Run to Him today.

- When you have seasons of suffering, remember your first love. Receive His redemption in those moments.
- When you are trapped in the grasp of idolatry, remember your first love. Receive His redemption in those moments.
- When you are experiencing the Jezzies, remember your first love. Receive His redemption in those moments.
- When you feel like your purpose is lost, remember your first love. Receive His redemption in those moments.
- When you are afraid, remember your first love. Receive His redemption in those moments.
- When you are weary and your strength is gone and your faith feels frail, remember your first love. Receive His redemption in those moments.

A true Overcomer recognizes the need for repentance, not just persistence and courage. It's time to humble ourselves and dig deeper. It's time to become true overcomers so that we can sit at God's banquet table and enjoy what He can't wait to give us. I encourage you today, to take a moment to remember what it was like when you first met Jesus. When He first melted your heart and swept you off your feet. Remind yourself, and then ask for forgiveness.

Every time your spirit feels dry and parched, remember your first love. Abandon yourself to this love today. She who overcomes always remembers her first love.

Always.

•••

Dear Jesus,

Forgive me for forgetting you as my first love. Forgive me for abandoning you for silly things and rushing past you, leaving you out of my day. Remind me of our first days together; rekindle the fire in my heart for you. I love you. I need you. Continue to mold me into an Overcomer who daily seeks you first.

In Jesus' Name, Amen.

•••

If you've never embraced God's love before, and you're falling in love with Him for the first time, take a moment to say this prayer…

Dear Jesus,

I'm falling in love with you for the first time today. I don't understand everything about this love, all I know is that I can't survive without it. Forgive me for the disobedience and the years of sin that have piled up in my life and separated me from you. Come and work in my heart, renew my mind, and mold me Lord so that I can be a reflection of you. I give you my life and my love today, Jesus. Have your way in me!

In Jesus' Name, Amen.

TRUTH ABOUT ME STATEMENTS:

- The love of Jesus, and God's love for me, is enough.
- I choose to fix my eyes on Jesus and embrace Him as my first love.
- The joy of my salvation has been restored through Jesus Christ's love for me!
- Through Christ my mistakes have been redeemed.

PERSONAL REFLECTION TIME:

- In what ways have you forgotten your first love?
- How would you describe Jesus' love for you and your relationship with Him?
- Describe a time when His love for you swept you off your feet.
- What verses speak to your heart like personal love letters from Jesus?

RELATED WORDS OF LIFE TO STUDY:

"Therefore, since we are surrounded by such a great cloud of witnesses, let us throw off everything that hinders and the sin that so easily entangles. And let us run with perseverance the race marked out for us, 2 fixing our eyes on Jesus, the pioneer and perfecter of faith. For the joy set before him he endured the cross, scorning its shame, and sat down at the right hand of the throne of God." ~Hebrews 12:1-2, NIV

*"Restore to me the joy of your salvation and grant me a willing spirit, to sustain me." ~*Psalm 51:12, NIV

*"For God so loved the world that he gave his one and only Son, that whoever believes in him shall not perish but have eternal life." ~*John 3:16, NIV

*"Keep yourselves in God's love as you wait for the mercy of our Lord Jesus Christ to bring you to eternal life." ~*Jude 1:21, NIV

10

She Wears the Wardrobe of an Overcomer

~redeemed of weakness~

If you were to find me on Pinterest and search my boards, you would find one titled "Fabulous Outfits." It is here that I pin everything that I wish could be in my closet.

In this virtual closet board, there are fabulous sweater dresses, shirt dresses, skinny jeans with high heels, photos of full outfits pieced together, jackets, scarves of all sizes, boots, stiletto heels, strappy belts, ideas for hats, and even a shoe-ology guide so I always have the right shoe paired with the right outfit. On and on it goes, a never-ending closet to spur on inspiration for whatever fashion I feel like emulating on any given day. The board is packed with, as of right now, over five-hundred and twenty-one pins! (I feel like there should be more than that. I better take a few moments and window shop my way around Pinterest for a while. I'll be back soon with my point!)

●●●

Most girls love dressing up and wearing fashionable clothes. We already established in Chapter Four the shopping addictions that we gals can struggle with from time to time. We live in the information age where anything we want to know can be found in a few quick minutes with the swipe of a finger and a wireless connection. Anything we want to buy we can get with or without cash in hand, and it can be delivered to our doorstep within the week. We work to live the American Dream, and yet the more we get, the less we have of what really matters most.

Something's got to change.

The treasure chest of an overcomer is filled with priceless riches that can't be pinned on Pinterest or instantly ordered in a digital world. They are often unseen by the naked eye, yet more important and more valuable than all the money and material possessions this earthly world can give. John talks about these riches in Revelation 3:15-21, MSG:

"I know you inside and out, and find little to my liking. You're not cold, you're not hot—far better to be either cold or hot! You're stale. You're stagnant. You make me want to vomit. You brag, 'I'm rich, I've got it made, I need nothing from anyone,' oblivious that in fact you're a pitiful, blind beggar, threadbare and homeless.

Here's what I want you to do: Buy your gold from me, gold that's been through the refiner's fire. Then you'll be rich. Buy your clothes from me, clothes designed in Heaven. You've gone around half-naked long enough. And buy medicine for your eyes from me so you can see, really see.

The people I love, I call to account—prod and correct and guide so that they'll live at their best. Up on your feet, then! About face! Run after God!

Look at me. I stand at the door. I knock. If you hear me call and open the door, I'll come right in and sit down to supper with you. Conquerors will sit alongside me at the head table, just as I, having conquered, took the place of honor at the side of my Father. That's my gift to the conquerors!'

Did you catch it? Did you find the treasure? Let's dig for it together…

~ CHARACTER. FAITH. PERSISTENCE. COURAGE. ~

"Buy your gold from me, gold that's been through the refiner's fire. Then you'll be rich."

As I was reading through this, God spoke to my heart. He said, "The gold that's been through the refiner's fire symbolizes character, faith, persistence, and courage." We often sing about the refiner's fire in worship songs, but only when we've walked through it can we fully begin to understand it. Only then can we behold the beautiful "gold" that's on the other side.

The process of refining gold can give us some insight into how this works spiritually. The most common methods available use either chemicals or fire. The first method involves placing the gold in strong acids that dissolve the impurities. This process is effective, yet it does not bring about the best refinement. Placing the gold in fire, the second method available to purify gold, brings about a ninety-nine point ninety-nine percent purity. But it's a dangerous process.

Using fire for refinement requires the goldsmith to place the gold in flames exceeding temperatures of one-thousand, eight-hundred and thirty-two degrees Fahrenheit. As he does this, he must stay right beside the flames, keeping an eye on the gold. Can you imagine standing close to flames that hot? If he takes his eye off of the gold, he risks overheating it and ruining it. Throughout the process, he pulls the gold in and out of the flame, diligently shaping it. He knows the gold is purified when he can see his reflection in it.

Read that last sentence again: He knows the gold is purified when he can see his reflection in it. Doesn't that give you goose bumps and chills? Think about it. The goldsmith knows that the gold is refined because he can see his reflection in it. In the same way, God knows our hearts are refined when he can see *His* reflection in us!

Remember in Chapter Two when we talked about how we must be persistent during our seasons of suffering? That is refinement. In those seasons of suffering, God is keeping a close eye on us. He is shaping us through the fire of suffering. When we come out of the flames of that season with a stronger faith and persistence to keep going, we come out shining with His reflection!

Remember in Chapters Six, Seven, and Eight how we talked about embracing the courage to be authentic, face our fears, and keep going when things get hard and look uncertain? That is refinement. In those seasons of growing and not giving up, God is keeping a close eye on us. He is shaping us through those experiences. When we come out of the flames of those seasons with more courage and character than when we went in, we come out shining with His reflection!

The process of refinement can't be a fun one for the gold. I mean, if gold had feelings and could speak, it would probably cry and grumble each time it was placed in those hot flames! The process of refinement isn't fun for us either. It hurts. It stretches us. It burns off the impurities that keep us dirty and grimy. In the process, we might feel abandoned, hopeless, and even completely helpless. We don't always see that our goldsmith is right beside us because the flames are so bright that they block our vision. But He's there! And in the end, we come out ninety-nine point ninety-nine percent purified. In the end, it is worth it. Character. Faith. Boldness. Courage. Persistence. All of these things and more are the result of going through the Refiner's fire. No riches in the world can replace those qualities. They are the true riches that God is speaking about in these verses.

Now that we've identified what comes out of the process of refinement (and now that I've returned from my pinning excursion on Pinterest), it's time to talk about some fabulous accessories that God has put together for us to create the perfect outfit.

~ MY PINTEREST CLOSET IS FAKE, BUT MY SPIRITUAL WARDROBE IS REAL ~

"Buy your clothes from me, clothes designed in Heaven. You've gone around half-naked long enough."

Have you ever noticed that we often wear our weakness like a straight jacket? It binds us up and everyone can see it. We must cut these stark white belts of restriction off of us and put on an outfit much better suited for the beautiful women God has created us to be. One of strength!

It's time to put on the wardrobe of an overcomer.

So, about this Pinterest board I've been talking about. If you haven't yet gone into Pinterest, heed my warning now and stay away. Save yourself from the pinning trap! But if you must get dragged into it, then be forewarned that you'll reach a moment where you'll wish your Pinterest closet was, in fact, a real closet. I sure wish mine was.

Hours have been spent pinning leopard scarves, fun dresses, dazzling belts, and who knows what other wardrobe necessities into this fake, virtual closet of mine. It's great for inspiration, yes, but let's be honest: it's not a real closet! I can't pick out an outfit on Pinterest and choose to wear it if I haven't actually bought all the pieces. The outfit only becomes a real thing for me to wear when I go to the store, purchase every item, and bring it home and place it in the confines of my real closet.

In the same way, we can't put on our spiritual wardrobe if we haven't put all the pieces in our real spiritual wardrobe. All the pieces are there on display for us, but it's up to us to grab each piece, take the price tag off, and put on each item. God has specifically designed a fabulous wardrobe for those who aspire to overcome so we don't have to walk around spiritually naked any longer. It includes fashionable accessories such as a heart of compassion, kindness, and humility. He's even added some bling with sparkles like gentleness and patience! Not only that, He's given us a bulletproof vest of righteousness that puts the enemy's gear to shame.

Let's take a peak at each item in the overcomer's wardrobe so we can be sure to wear them every day. They really are the most important items we will ever put on!

1. The first item is the Belt of Truth.

Girl, strap that belt on as tight as you can because there will be moments where the lies and labels that we discussed in Chapter Seven will try to steal it away from you. As you can about imagine, this belt doesn't exactly go around our waists. No, it actually goes around our hearts and our minds. It keeps us secure and holds all of the other accessories of the spiritual wardrobe in place. We must stand firm in the truth each and every day.

2. Second is the Breastplate of Righteousness.

(a.k.a. the most fabulous bulletproof vest ever designed!) The purpose of a breastplate and a bulletproof vest is to protect our vital organs in combat situations. With this securely in place, we find the boldness to step out and conquer territories that would otherwise make us cower in fear without it. Confidence and boldness comes when we know who we are in Christ and are secure in our righteousness. Strap on that bulletproof vest, my friend. Wear it proudly and be bold!

3. Of course we can't forget our shoes.

After all, shoes are one of the most important pieces of any outfit! These shoes are a bit different than your average pair though. These shoes fit your feet perfectly, but they each have a different word written on them. The right shoe says "Readiness," and the left one says "Peace." When we wear these shoes, we are able to foster an atmosphere and attitude of peace. We are also fully equipped and ready to be used of God in every situation.

4. We must remember our Shield of Faith.

Think of it like a beautiful, fireproof umbrella with strength of steel that you hold up to keep you from getting drenched in the rain of doubt and despair. Pull it out and shield yourself with it when the flaming arrows of the enemy come flying at you. Carry it with you at all times, even when the sun is shining. Have enough faith to see things that others can't see and always be ready!

5. The next accessory that is essential is the Helmet of Salvation.

Now, I'm not a big fan of helmets, because they mess up my hair! So I like to think of this helmet more like a hat that protects your mind from the lies and labels that the enemy tries to distract you with. When you have the helmet of salvation on, you are able to shut the door on doubt and know that your salvation is secure in Jesus.

6. Finally, we need our weapon.

Yes, girl, this outfit requires a weapon – the Sword of the Spirit, also known as God's Word. Carry this weapon like a great female spy would carry a vibrant tube of red lipstick embedded with a secret knife that is laced with deadly venom. (I just love spy shows!) When you bring this sword out – i.e., you speak it and let the words roll off your lips – it cuts through the lies and brings life to all who hear it. As with any weapon, you must learn how to use it well. So study God's word daily. Diligently work at applying it every day. Write it on your heart in the morning and throughout the day. When you do, you'll be fully equipped to use it as the weapon it is designed to be!

A bonus accessory that we must not neglect is prayer. It is an essential part of overcoming anything! The Message version of the Bible describes all of these items of the spiritual wardrobe in the following way:

"Be prepared. You're up against far more than you can handle on your own. Take all the help you can get, every weapon God has issued, so that when it's all over but the shouting you'll still be on your feet. Truth, righteousness, peace, faith, and salvation are more than words. Learn how to apply them. You'll need them throughout your life. God's Word is an indispensable weapon. In the same way, prayer is essential in this ongoing warfare. Pray hard and long. Pray for your brothers and sisters. Keep your eyes open. Keep each other's spirits up so that no one falls behind or drops out." ~Ephesians 6:10-18, MSG

I encourage you to study the full armor of God until you understand it enough to put it on each and every day. Ask God to reveal the hidden meanings to you and how you can apply this in your own life starting this week!

~ DO YOU SEE WHAT I SEE? ~

"And buy medicine for your eyes from me so you can see, really see."

When we choose to listen to God and go after the treasure of strengthening our spiritual eyes so we can see what God sees, crazy things happen. We begin to overcome in new ways because we see things in a new light.

I can best describe this by sharing with you the revelation that God gave me through a string of prophetic dreams. During a twenty-one day spiritual fast, God spoke to me through several dreams that all had to do with my eyes. The first two dreams took place in war zones, and I kept getting my eyes covered with mud or chemicals. The last thing that happened in each dream was an explosion that covered my eyes, leaving me with a sense of desperation and defeat. I would wake up wondering what was going on, sensing in my spirit that these dreams were about some sort of spiritual warfare I was either already in or about to enter.

The last dream I had involved my searching for a very

expensive brand of mascara at a party. Mascara, of all things! This dream was clearly not about any type of warfare; however, the similar theme of eyes couldn't be ignored. There was something that God was trying to tell me.

In this dream, I was at a very distinguished party in a mansion. The clinking of wine glasses could be heard beneath the hum of guests laughing and talking. Somewhere in another room the beat of the bass could be heard, inviting people to dance. I strolled through each room, admiring the stark modern décor of white, black, and red. In my heart I had a sense of urgency, so I kept winding through the house even though I noticed celebrities and friends that I wanted to talk to. The glitz and glamour of this place was like nothing I had ever seen before, and it was difficult not to be distracted by it.

I found myself wandering up a beautiful, winding staircase that was positioned in the foyer where a dazzling crystal chandelier hung from the ceiling. At the top of the stairs I saw a booth, and in this booth was a display of makeup. Sitting on the top of the table was the silver tube of mascara that I had been searching for all night long. I began walking toward it, and then suddenly I woke up.

My first thought upon waking from this strange slumber was, "Okay, God, are you trying to tell me to start taking off my eye makeup at night?" (If you're a beauty expert, don't hate me! Taking better care of my skin and face is a work in progress for me.) It really didn't make sense! All morning I thought about this dream and wondered what was wrong with my brain to care so much about makeup that it showed up in my dreams.

I walked into the bathroom and began getting ready for the day. As I was putting the final touches of makeup on my face, I found myself in a conversation with God about the meaning of this dream. He asked me, "Mandy, what does mascara do?"

"Well," I replied out loud, "it defines your eyes." (Yes, I talk to God out loud when I'm alone.)

"Right," He said. "Mandy, I'm defining your spiritual eyes

during this time so that you can see things in a new light!"

Suddenly all three of these prophetic dreams made sense to me, and the mystery of the mascara and covered eyes was revealed.

Sometimes our spiritual eyesight is weak. When we aren't conditioned to see things by faith, or we don't take the time to ask God for clarification, we miss what God is trying to reveal to us. It takes a trained eye to see it. We must activate persistence in strengthening our spiritual eyes. We must be courageous and willing to look at things through a new lens. We must be willing to "buy medicine for our eyes" from God so we really can begin to see!

The wardrobe of an overcomer is filled with character, faith, persistence, courage - all of those important accessories known as the full armor of God - righteousness....and a strengthened eyesight that only comes from God. They all work together and are important tools that we need in order to be victorious and overcome.

But the reality is that sometimes we miss the mark because of our own weakness and lack of spiritual maturity. In those situations, we must recognize that God is redeeming our weakness and correcting us because He loves us enough to do so, just like He mentions in Revelation 3:15-21.

~ REDEEMED OF WEAKNESS ~

"The people I love, I call to account—prod and correct and guide so that they'll live at their best. Up on your feet, then! About face! Run after God!"

Have you ever have one of those mornings?

Maybe the kids woke up sick, or you spilled your coffee all over the kitchen floor, and then your fluffy white puppy pranced through it spreading coffee sludge footprints all over the house. Or maybe you can relate to the way one of my Friday mornings started out...

Normally when I wake up, the first thing I do is strap myself into my vest for a thirty minute breathing treatment. That's where I pull out my Bible, journal, and a colored pen to spend time with God. This is what sets the course for my day – it gets my heart right, helps my mind focus on truth, and keeps my attitude chipper. However, on this particular Friday morning, my routine was out of sorts due to some blood work that I needed to have done at the clinic. So, I quickly got out of bed, threw my hair up in a bun, put on my workout clothes, and left the apartment. (Apparently all of my spiritual accessories were left behind in a pile on the floor, and my spiritual eyesight was blurry and filled with that icky crusty sleep.) My plan was to get to the clinic, do the blood work, and then get back home to do my treatment, spend time with God and shower. All of this was going to take no more than an hour tops. That was my plan.

Things rarely go exactly as planned.

The blood work I had to do was a glucose test – the fasting one where you go in super hungry and can't eat until it's over, and in between the pricks and pokes they make you drink a sugary orange liquid that at first tastes like orange pop but quickly becomes disgusting. This is a yearly test for me since I have cystic fibrosis, and CFRD (CF related diabetes) is something that often develops.

The first thing I noticed when I entered the lab was that Jan was not behind the reception desk. She was the receptionist who had been there since I was a kid, and I always looked forward to chatting with her. Today there was no Jan. Instead, there was a very flustered Phlebotomist behind the computer trying to check patients in, answer the phone, do paperwork, and all other tasks that clearly were NOT her cup of tea, based on her facial expression. She looked up at me, checked me in, and very sharply tried to explain the glucose test to me. (It felt like she was trying to explain it to herself more than me because she really wasn't talking to me, but at me.) I shrugged it off and smiled, then took my seat in the waiting room. Shortly after that, my name was called and my blood was taken by a much friendlier Phlebotomist. That was at 8:15 A.M.

I was told to hang around in the waiting room until they were called with some blood levels so they knew how much juice to give me. So, there I sat.

8:25 A.M...

8:30 A.M...

8:45 A.M...

As the minutes ticked by, my patience and anxiety began to rise. Now, I must warn you, this is the part of the story where the evidence of my spiritual nakedness shows up. I'm not proud of it.

It had been forty minutes by the time I stood up, and no one had addressed this fact even though we established eye contact several times. So I walked over to the desk, and before I could open my mouth, the Rude One looked at me and said, "Our system is down so we had to send someone over to a different lab for the results. It's going to be...a while." Then she glared at me.

Now, I'm not proud of this, but I didn't spend time with God that morning, and, like I said, I was in my gym clothes with my hair in a bun with no spiritual accessories adorning my sloppy outfit, so I was slightly depleted in my patience/kindness tank. I mumbled a sarcastic comment, something along the lines of, "So, basically my morning is shot then. Great. Okay – thanks." And then I glared back at her with a fake smile.

I took a deep breath and walked back to my seat, pulled out my phone, and opened up my Kindle app to read the Bible. (Apparently I knew my attitude was not very Christ-like in that moment and felt the need for an intervention.)

As I was thumbing through the pages looking for Psalms, I felt a nudge. Have you ever felt a nudge after you've said something you shouldn't? Well, I felt a nudge. And then I heard God say to me, "Patience. They will know me by your actions." Immediately I realized that my actions in that moment weren't exactly shining

God's glory. So I had a come to Jesus moment and continued talking to Him.

And do you know what He did? He had me wait there for FORTY MORE MINUTES!! Yeah! Oh yes He did! Even though I wasn't initially thrilled with this, I began to see the opportunity that He had placed right in front of me in the midst of my impatience. With the gentle nudge to read His word, and by opening up my time to do so right then and there, He began the process of redeeming the weak areas of my heart that had indulged in selfishness, irritability, and rudeness. His words brought conviction and eventually forgiveness and repentance. He was prodding, correcting, and guiding me so that I could be my best!

By the end of that morning, I had a renewed attitude. I was able to identify how important our spiritual wardrobe really is and what happens when we don't put even a few pieces on each day. For instance, because I forgot my belt of truth, the lies began screaming in my head as I waited and waited and waited and waited that day. The lies said, "You're so impatient. What a selfish person you are. You're a horrible example to others, and they just forgot about you on purpose." None of those things were the truth. I am not a selfish, impatient, horrible example of a person, and they didn't forget about me. I was, however, a person who had a moment of weakness and displayed some attitudes that weren't quite right.

If I would have had my feet fitted with the right shoes, I would have been able to walk in peace and been ready with patient words and actions. But I wasn't. Nope. Not. At. All. There was clearly no peace to be found anywhere around me that morning! At least not until I opened God's word and let Him begin the redemption process on my weaknesses.

Maybe you can relate to this feeling? We don't always get it right. We are human and sometimes we give in to our human emotions instead of the spiritual prompting from our Heavenly Father. What we put on each day, and how we see things, is so important! It impacts the world around us more than we realize.

Overcomers allow God to redeem their weaknesses. They aren't satisfied with anything less than true riches. They seek out God's treasure chest filled with true riches like refined gold, a spiritual wardrobe, and strengthened spiritual eyesight. My friend, it's time for us to stop chasing the American Dream and start going after God's dream. It's time to quit gazing in our Pinterest closet with a look of longing and grab hold of the spiritual wardrobe right in front of us. He designed us to overcome the powers of darkness and deception, and He's fully equipped us to do so successfully.

•••

Dear Jesus,

I come to you today to ask you for forgiveness for the times when I have been stagnant and stale with you. Lord, help me to be on fire for you! Jesus, I want to be refined so that I can come out with a stronger faith and boldness in you. Help me to wear your fashionable wardrobe every day, and strengthen my spiritual eyes so I can see what you want to show me. My greatest desire is to become the Overcomer that you've designed me to be. Thank you, Lord, for loving me enough to get my attention so I can grow deeper in my relationship with you.

In Jesus' name, Amen

TRUTH ABOUT ME STATEMENTS:

- I am rich because God has refined me.
- I choose to put on the full armor of God daily, which is the wardrobe of an overcomer.

- My spiritual eyesight is being strengthened and I have eyes to see what God wants to reveal to me.
- I have been redeemed of my weaknesses.

PERSONAL REFLECTION TIME:

- Would you describe your relationship with God as hot, cold, or stagnant and stale?
- What did God reveal to you in this chapter?
- In what ways has God brought you through a Refiner's Fire?
- Describe the character, faith, persistence, and courage that are evident in your life right now.
- How can you put on God's wardrobe this week?
- Would you describe your spiritual eyesight as weak, strong, or completely blind?

RELATED WORDS OF LIFE TO STUDY:

"The night is almost gone, and the day is near. Therefore let us lay aside the deeds of darkness and put on the armor of light." ~ Romans 13:12

"So, as those who have been chosen of God, holy and beloved, put on a heart of compassion, kindness, humility, gentleness and patience." ~ Colossians 3:12

"You younger men, likewise, be subject to your elders; and all of you, clothe yourselves with humility toward one another, for God is opposed to the proud, but gives grace to the humble." ~ 1 Peter 5:5

"So, as those who have been chosen of God, holy and beloved, put on a heart of compassion, kindness, humility, gentleness and patience; bearing with one another, and forgiving each other, whoever has a complaint against anyone; just as the Lord forgave you, so also should you. Beyond all these things put on love, which is the perfect bond of unity." ~ Colossians 3:12-14

"Put on the full armor of God, so that you will be able to stand firm against the schemes of the devil. For our struggle is not against flesh and blood, but against the rulers, against the powers, against the world forces of this darkness, against the spiritual forces of wickedness in the heavenly places. Therefore, take up the full armor of God, so that you will be able to resist in the evil day, and having done everything, to stand firm. Stand firm therefore, having girded your loins with truth, and having put on the breastplate of righteousness, and having shod your feet with the preparation of the gospel of peace; in addition to all, taking up the shield of faith with which you will be able to extinguish all the flaming arrows of the evil one. And take the helmet of salvation, and the sword of the Spirit, which is the word of God. With all prayer and petition pray at all times in the Spirit, and with this in view, be on the alert with all perseverance and petition for all the saints." ~ Ephesians 6:11-18

"He will sit as a refiner and purifier of silver; he will purify the Levites and refine them like gold and silver. Then the LORD will have men who will bring offerings in righteousness..." ~Malachi 3:3, NIV

11

She has a Heart of Gratitude and Walks with Grace

~redeemed of uncertainty~

~ BLESS THESE YELLOW WALLS ~

The apartment was quiet except for the lingering notes of soft piano music in the background. Lights were low, the Christmas tree twinkled, and I sat with my legs crossed on our couch with a warm cup of coffee resting between my hands. Ajah B. had finally found a cozy position after circling around several times on the orange blanket beside me. It was a beautiful, serene moment that begged me to pause before family and friends arrived for the holidays.

I sat there in silence, listening to the music, and for the first time in four years I felt content. Truly content and extremely grateful beyond words.

The yellow walls of our apartment had always been a sore

spot for me. It took me a good year before I realized why – they were the exact color of the walls in the Galleria apartment that burned down. Once that realization hit my heart, I began to loathe the apartment we had moved into. Through the years of depression and sickness, I always felt that the yellow walls of our home were nothing but a horrible reminder of all that was lost.

However, on this beautiful day right before Christmas, I saw our yellow walls in a different light. No longer bare, resembling a cave, they were now decorated with colorful pictures that displayed the inspirational words of life my heart had needed to see. Family photos hung on the walls, and the home décor was finally beginning to resemble life again.

My heart was suddenly bursting with gratitude for everything that we had gone through to get us to this place – this home with yellowed walls that had been filled with so much struggle, persistence, courage, and redemption. These yellow walls that told the story of overcoming depression and sickness. These yellow walls that held the secrets of my darkest moments. This was the moment that I finally saw these yellow walls through the eyes of gratitude instead of resentment.

I stood up, turned the music on louder, and began to praise God for these yellow walls. I asked Him to bless them, and I thanked Him for the years of struggle that happened within these walls that had become our home. It was a beautiful, full circle moment that I had not planned on ever experiencing. Oh, how glad I am that I have that particular moment embedded in my heart to cherish forever!

~ BEGIN WITH GRATITUDE ~

One beautiful moment of gratitude and contentment won't last a lifetime. We must choose to see things through the lens of gratitude every day.

The other morning I woke up in a funk. Has that ever happened to you? As I was doing my treatment, I felt God nudge my heart. He inspired me right then and there to journal twenty-five things that I was grateful for that morning. You know what happened next? I found myself smiling with each sentence I wrote! My day turned around before I even got dressed, and the things that had been piling up in the back of my mind all week ceased to bother me.

Gratitude. It is a powerful tool that God has blessed us with to help us choose our attitudes no matter what we are facing each day. Once I finished my list of twenty-five things, I turned the page and wrote a quick poem. I pray that it encourages you today and helps you take your pen to paper to record your own list of thankfulness.

When you begin the morning
With gratitude,
You paint a beautiful day!

It refreshes your soul,
Redirects your mind,
And sets your heart on course.

It paints a smile on your face,
A sparkle in your eye,
And a soothing sound in your voice.

"A thankful heart,"
"An attitude of gratitude,"
Or "count your blessings," you say.

Whatever you call it the fact remains,
When you're thankful,
It's a beautiful day!

We always get what we focus on. Overcomers know that the best way to shift their perspective in life is to practice the skill of gratitude. Not only does being thankful help your disposition, it also brings with it a handful of other benefits:

1. Gratitude Improves Your Health.

Have you been experiencing some restless nights lately? Maybe it's the same routine every evening – you fall into bed exhausted, ready to drift off only to find that your mind runs wild with worry just as your head hits the pillow. You worry about tomorrow's "to-do" list, your daughter's medication, your husband's job and how you're ever going to create a quality future for your kids, let alone yourself. Just before you drift off you're hit with a crippling fear that right around the corner lays a sleeping giant – a car accident, house fire, or bad doctor appointment – all of which seem to be inevitable in your mind.

Friend, if any part of this resonates within you, it's time to step up and choose something different!

Gratitude.

Studies show that those who practice gratitude on a regular basis sleep better and recover faster from illness than those who do not. Gratitude helps improve mental health, including depression and anxiety, as well as addictive behaviors. Not to mention the fact that gratitude makes you happy, and who wouldn't like to be more happy?! Just do a search on the Internet of "the effects of gratitude on health." You'll discover tons of information on this subject.

2. Gratitude Improves Your Relationships.

I've personally experienced this in my marriage as well as other relationships. Being thankful opens the door to being genuine. My marriage has been strengthened because my husband and I express gratitude toward each other daily.

My friendship with my best friends is stronger because we express gratitude for both moments of extreme happiness, as well as those moments of pure honesty where we sit down for a "come to Jesus moment!" (This has happened on many occasions on the actual big blue couch and my two best gals and I have each been on the receiving end of a healthy dose of truth!)

Being grateful allows others to see your heart and the depth of your emotions. Yes, it means being vulnerable…but it's worth it every time.

3. Gratitude Is A Spiritual Discipline.

It's true. Our natural human tendency is not to be grateful. I don't know if you've noticed, but the human race can be downright wicked.

That's where the spiritual discipline of gratitude comes in. It's not easy or normal to be thankful when bad things happen; however, it is the fastest way to shift your perspective and let God chisel you in the midst of your circumstances. Practicing gratitude in everything – in every situation whether good or bad, healthy or sick, rich or poor, happy or sad – is a spiritual act of obedience that we are all called to walk in.

In everything give thanks…

- on good days
- on lonely days
- in times of debt and financial crisis
- on sad days
- while yearning for a baby
- when struggling to breathe
- while doing treatments
- during panic attacks
- in depression
- in grief
- in joy
- while singing
- while playing piano
- while loving and eventually losing a family pet
- while loving your spouse
- in sickness and in health

- in happy times with friends
- in moments of fear
- while working
- on social media
- while running
- in yoga class
- when laughing
- in times when God is silent
- in times where it feels God isn't there.

In every situation we find ourselves in, we are called to give thanks.

~ REDEEMED OF UNCERTAINTY ~

Gratitude helps you move your thoughts from uncertainty about the future to faith and certainty in Christ's ability to work in your life for His good! It's all about perspective!

What are you grateful for today? Actually, maybe a better question to start with is what have you been uncertain about lately? Take a moment to think about that. Now, within the uncertainties, what can you find to be thankful for or about?

When we shift our perspective and have a heart of gratitude even in the hardest of times, we begin to see that God is rescuing us from all of our worries and uncertainties. He redeems them! Let's allow God to walk us through this process of redeeming our uncertainties in regards to what we have learned in this book during our time together so far...

- What are the current "ashes" in your life, and in what ways can you express gratitude in the midst of them? (Chapter One)
- How can you have a heart of gratitude toward the suffering that you've endured? (Chapter Two)

- In what ways can you be thankful for the times that you've been weary? (Chapter Three)
- How has discovering the hidden idols in your life made you more thankful? (Chapter Four)
- In what ways can you be thankful for the Jezzies in your life? (Chapter Five)
- When it comes to finding your purpose and living authentically, what are you thankful for? (Chapter Six)
- In what ways are you thankful for the lies, labels, and fears that you've experienced and overcome? (Chapter Seven)
- What doors has God shut for you that you are thankful for? What doors has He opened that you are thankful for? (Chapter Eight)
- When it comes to remembering your first love, what are you thankful for? (Chapter Nine)
- What refining process have you been through, and how has it made you more grateful? (Chapter Ten)

Answering these questions helps you shift your perspective from one of uncertainty to one of gratitude. Take the time to sit with God this week and let Him redeem all of your uncertainties through His word and this journaling process.

~ THE FIVE STEPS OF GRACE ~

Finally, we must take a few moments to focus on the topic of grace. We won't be victorious overcomers without it.

In the early fall of 2014 I put myself on a thirty-day challenge. A no latte challenge to be exact. I wanted to inspire others to get healthier while cutting back on my favorite beverage. It was easier than I thought, until I got to day twenty-five. That was the day that Raychel and I took a therapeutic road trip to hold each other accountable and deal with some emotions and beliefs from our pasts that were keeping us stuck. We always say we are nothing if not real, so we have to practice what we preach! This particular day brought us to two different cemeteries, a park bench, and a football field all in a total of seven hours and just over two-hundred and forty miles. It was emotional. Exhausting. Liberating. And the kind of trip that requires nostalgic comfort. So yes, I cracked and chose to embrace a grande soy caramel macchiato at the beginning of the day. Ugh! To be honest, in that moment I felt like such a failure and a horrible health coach. And that's exactly the moment that a small, five-letter word whispered across my heart.

Grace.

It's something I teach my clients to extend to themselves. I remind them often and reassure them that they are doing the best they can, and that's good enough. I remind them that mistakes are to be expected and not to beat themselves up about it. At work, I do this. With my clients, I do this. Yet, I often forget to give it to myself. I am my own worst critic. Maybe you can relate?

The dictionary defines grace in many ways – here are two of them:

- a manifestation of favor, especially by a superior *(a.k.a. forgiveness, charity, and mercifulness.)*
- mercy; clemency; pardon

How many times do we struggle with giving ourselves forgiveness, favor, or mercy? Based on my line of work, I'd say it's more times than we can count! But there is a better way. We can choose GRACE instead of perfection. I'm thankful for day twenty-five of that challenge because without it, I wouldn't have discovered the *Five Steps of GRACE* that all overcomers must embrace.

Let's briefly review each letter in this acronym…

G = Gain Perspective.

Giving ourselves grace requires that we gain some perspective. Perspective on where we are at, where we came from, and where we want to go. Making a mistake doesn't make us bad people. It simply means that there is an opportunity for more growth. When we encounter moments where grace is needed, it's the perfect opportunity to choose to see things in a new light.

R = Release the Guilt.

Giving ourselves grace requires us to release the guilt. There's no such thing as perfect people. Perfection is unattainable, so do yourself a favor and release yourself from the guilt of not measuring up to other people's standards. Release yourself from the guilt of making mistakes. You are good enough right now. In this moment. Not because I say so, but because God says so. He sees who you are now and who you are becoming. And guess what? He loves you through it all. So let it go. Guilt only holds you back from the amazing things waiting in your future. Release it and be done with it for good!

A = Allow Your Body to Rest and Relax.

Giving ourselves grace requires us to allow our bodies to rest and relax. Yes, it is similar to the A in PAUSE because it is that important! We run out of steam when we push ourselves too hard. Rest and relaxation are great ways to recharge not only our bodies, but also our weary souls and fragile emotions. The tension of perfectionism takes a toll on us physically, mentally, and spiritually so give yourself some grace this week to rest and relax.

C = Choose to Forgive.

Giving ourselves grace requires us to choose forgiveness. Forgiveness toward others, yes, but mostly forgiveness toward ourselves. Make it a habit to forgive yourself when you let yourself down. Recognize what you're doing right and celebrate that while letting go of the pressure that you place on yourself. Forgiveness heals. Forgiveness matters. So choose to forgive.

E = Embrace Truth.

Giving ourselves grace requires us to embrace truth. First, embrace God's truth of who He says you are. He says you are whole, holy, free, energetic, and strong! (Ephesians 1:1-19, MSG) Begin embracing *that* truth and then begin to embrace the truth of your situation. If we don't face the truth of where we are right now, we can't move forward in the right direction. It's impossible! So embrace the truth because the truth will always set you free.

•••

She who overcomes works diligently to have a heart of gratitude, knowing that God alone is in charge of redeeming all of her uncertainties as she applies it. And when she makes a mistake, she holds her head up high and walks with the grace that has been given to her.

TRUTH ABOUT ME STATEMENTS:

- I have a heart of gratitude.
- I choose to be thankful in every situation.
- When I make a mistake, or fall short of my goals, I will extend grace to myself.
- I will extend grace to others just as Christ has extended it to me.

PERSONAL REFLECTION TIME:

- Do you find expressing gratitude to be an easy or a hard thing for you to do? Why?

- Write down ten things that you are thankful for today. Keep doing this every day by starting a Gratitude Journal.
- In what ways do you need to apply grace to your life this week?
- In what ways do you need to extend grace to others?

RELATED WORDS OF LIFE TO STUDY:

"Rejoice always, pray continually, give thanks in all circumstances; for this is God's will for you in Christ Jesus." ~1 Thessalonians 5:16-18, NIV

"See to it that no one falls short of the grace of God and that no bitter root grows up to cause trouble and defile many." ~Hebrews 12:15, NIV

"And the God of all grace, who called you to his eternal glory in Christ, after you have suffered a little while, will himself restore you and make you strong, firm and steadfast." ~1 Peter 5:10, NIV

CONCLUSION
She Who Overcomes is Beautifully Whole

Overcoming something - anything - takes time. It can't be rushed, nor should it be.

For four long years after the fire, I was held captive by fear. Fear of losing again. Fear of another traumatic event. Fear of having to start over yet again because of another fire. Fires and flames instantly took me back to that day in 2010. I avoided being near an open flame of any kind and returned or re-gifted any candle that I was given. The risk was too high for me. It's a miracle that I even used our oven at all, especially since a pizza once caused oven flames to spark in our first apartment after the fire!

Recently, on a beautiful fall afternoon, I found myself in the candle aisle at Target. My hand reached out and grabbed something that it had not touched for eons. I held the candle in my hand and examined it carefully. It was larger than the tea lights that had been on my shopping list that day. This candle made a statement. It was aesthetically pleasing, yes, but that's not what drew me to it. Confident. Brave. Whole. Those were the words that danced upon my heart as I placed this new treasure in our shopping cart.

"Today is the day, Nate. I'm ready," I explained to my husband.

His reply was laced with the gentle words of a loving husband who understood well the journey his wife had traveled. "I'm proud of you," he said with a smile.

...

We've just traveled through a beautiful journey together, you and I. It's been filled with many life lessons and tough questions. We've trained our brains to find the truth in the midst of the lies. And we've come out on the other side...beautifully whole.

Becoming beautifully whole is a process. You can't just wake up one day and decide to be whole. It requires authenticity, vulnerability, persistence, courage, and the ability to receive the gift of redemption that Jesus paid for on the cross. That doesn't happen in a day, a month, or even in a year. It's a process; a beautiful, delicate process that is worth every moment of suffering in the ashes along the way.

~ BEAUTY OUT OF ASHES ~

When we first see the ashes, our minds travel through a frenzy of bad memories. We question how it got to this point. We feel insecure, threatened, and unsafe. In the midst of the chaos and pain, we can't see the sprouts within the ashes – the richness that is growing because of them.

Ashes are rich potting soil. The Hawaiian Islands are covered with some of the most beautiful and exotic plants and flowers that have ever graced the earth. Why? Because the Hawaiian Islands have soil that is heavy with volcanic ash. This heavy soil filled with ashes has helped nourish and fertilize the beautiful plants that have since emerged.

When wild fires destroy forests, everything is covered in thick blackness. For months the ground looks barren. Cold. Dead. But give it enough time and eventually some rare flowers and plants will begin to emerge, showing the beauty that was hidden in the devastation.

Ashes are rich potting soil that paves the way for small, beautiful sprouts to grow.

I didn't know the beauty that would emerge on the other side of those slippery ashes back in 2010. I didn't realize what was being burned off of me. But through the process of learning how to persist, embracing courage that I never knew I had, and receiving the redemption that Jesus so graciously held out for me, I have emerged on the other side of those ashes a stronger woman.

Ashes are rich potting soil that paves the way for small, beautiful sprouts to grow in the midst of our circumstances. Sprouts of bravery, faith, courage, persistence, strength, authenticity, vulnerability, character, truth, redemption, and wholeness. Beautiful wholeness.

Be persistent, my friend. Be courageous. Receive the redemption that God has for you. Make the decision to be a "she who overcomes" no matter what.

•••

There is a moment in your future, possibly right around the corner, where you will look in the mirror and see just how beautifully whole you have become. It is already written! My prayer for you is that as you close this book, you will make the choice to be an overcomer and rise out of the ashes of your circumstances.

TRUTH ABOUT ME STATEMENT:

- I am beautifully whole.

RELATED WORDS OF LIFE TO STUDY:

"The Spirit of the Sovereign Lord is on me, because the Lord has anointed me to preach good news to the poor. He has sent me to bind up the brokenhearted, to proclaim freedom for the captives and release from darkness for the prisoners, 2 to proclaim the year of the Lord's favor and the day of vengeance of our God, to comfort all who mourn, 3 and provide for those who grieve in Zion-- to bestow on them a crown of beauty instead of ashes, the oil of gladness instead of mourning, and a garment of praise instead of a spirit of despair. They will be called oaks of righteousness, a planting of the LORD for the display of his splendor."
~Isaiah 61:1-3, NIV

LIFE COACHING

TOOL BOX

CHAPTER RECAP:

Let's recap the tools we have gathered on this journey of becoming overcomers and rising out of the ashes in the midst of chaos and pain.

1

We discovered the ashes in our lives that God wants to help us rise up out of.

2

We discovered how to persist during suffering. We must be brave and walk by faith.

3

We discovered the importance of rest and The Art of the PAUSE:

P= Pay attention to your emotions.

A= Allow time to rest.

U= Utilize stolen moments.

S= Say no!

E= Embrace the truth that you are worth it.

4

We discovered how to persist in getting rid of the things that hold us back. We must constantly identify the forms of idolatry that might be lurking within our hearts and take a stand for truth, righteousness, and Godliness.

5

We identified the Jezzie behaviors in our own lives and discovered the Honor Code of Conflict Resolution (a.k.a The Five Steps to Dealing with the Jezzies).

1. Let the dust settle.
2. Look in the mirror.
3. Extend grace and forgiveness.
4. Seek to understand the other person.
5. Establish new behaviors.

6

We discovered the courage to be authentic and journeyed through the tough questions to help find our purpose.

7

We found the courage to face the lies, labels, and fears that kept us stuck. We faced the truth that it takes courage to be weak so God can then be strong, and focused on three ways to confront the fear.

1. Feel it and confess it.
2. Speak with authority.
3. Put it in writing.

8

We found the courage to look crazy and walk by faith no matter what. We also discovered what to do when things don't turn out the way we had hoped or prayed they would.

9

We identified how to recognize when we have lost our first love and what to do to get back on track.

10

We discovered what happens during the refining process and why it is important. We also identified the pieces of our spiritual wardrobe and how to strengthen our spiritual eyesight.

11

We discovered how to shift our perspective from uncertainty and worry to one of gratitude. We also discovered the Five Steps of GRACE:

G = Gain perspective.

R = Release the guilt.

A = Allow your body to rest and relax.

C = Choose to forgive.

E = Embrace truth.

TRUTH ABOUT ME STATEMENTS ARCHIVE:

- I was born to overcome every challenge that stands in my way.

- With God's help, I can become an overcomer!

- I am brave because God says I am and makes it so.

- I am fearless!

- I am steadfast.

- I trust the Lord.

- I am secure in the Lord.

- I am able to walk by faith because God equips me and calls me to it.

- I will look for the sprouts that God has for me in every difficult circumstance.

- I believe that I am worthy of the rest God wants to give to me.

- When I am weary, I bring my burdens to God and He gives me rest.

- I am able to schedule a day of rest once a week.

- I am dedicated to refreshing, relaxing, and recharging my mind, body, and soul so that I can be the overcomer God has designed me to be.

- I am capable of learning and applying the art of the PAUSE, knowing that when I do, God's voice will become loud and clear.

- I stand firm in my faith.

- I am able to rise above idolatry and not give in to it from this point forward!

- I am made new in Christ, therefore my past addictions can be overcome.

- I will not deny Christ, but I will stand up for truth and righteousness.

- I refuse to operate in the behaviors of the Jezebel Spirit (a.k.a. The Jezzies).

- When someone hurts me, I will choose to forgive him or her.

- I have the courage to resolve conflict with honor.

- I have been revived and set free!

- The calling on my life is good enough because God says it is. He is the Qualifier and He says I am qualified!

- I have been equipped with everything I need to accomplish the calling God has placed on my life.

- I have no fear of bad news. My heart is steadfast and I trust in the Lord.

- I am not the labels that other people have put on me, or that I have put on myself. I am courageous and fearless!

- I have authority to overcome the power of the enemy, as well as the lies, labels, and fears that have been stopping me.

- I am a courageous overcomer.

- When I am weak, He is strong!

- I am a woman of bondage breaking faith.

- I am brave enough to keep going, even when I'm weary, even when I feel as though others think I'm crazy.

- I will hold on to God's truth in every situation.

- I will look to God, and for God, in every situation.

- I will use the strength that I do have to hold on when I am weary.

- The love of Jesus, and God's love for me, is enough.

- I choose to fix my eyes on Jesus and embrace him as my first love.

- The joy of my salvation has been restored through Jesus Christ's love for me!

- Through Christ my mistakes have been redeemed.

- I am rich because God has refined me.

- I choose to put on the full armor of God daily, which is the wardrobe of an overcomer.

- My spiritual eyesight is being strengthened and I have eyes to see what God wants to reveal to me.

- I have been redeemed of my weaknesses.

- I have a heart of gratitude.

- I choose to be thankful in every situation.

- When I make a mistake, or fall short of my goals, I will extend grace to myself.

- I will extend grace to others just as Christ has extended it to me.

- I am beautifully whole.

PERSONAL REFLECTION QUESTIONS ARCHIVE:

1

- As you read Mandy's story, what challenging circumstances came to your mind from your own life?
- How has God worked through these hard times?
- In what ways has God shown you that you are already an overcomer? Write them down. If this is difficult for you, ask God to reveal them to you and spend some quiet time in His loving arms.
- What are some of the current "ashes" in your life that God wants to help you rise up out of?

2

- Identify where you are in your journey by answering the following questions:
  - o Are you in a season of suffering and holding on to your faith? If so, describe what that has been like.
  - o Are you on the other side of suffering, walking as an overcomer who is already victorious? If so, write down the sprouts that came out of those ashes (a.k.a. the miracles that God did in the midst of the suffering).
- What has God taught you in your past seasons of suffering?
- Take a few moments to journal and ask God for wisdom in the current season that you are walking through. Ask Him to show you where you need to persist and endure.

3

- What habits and/or thoughts wear you out?
- When you feel emotionally and spiritually exhausted, what do you tend to do?
- What habits help you persist when you feel weary?
- What does letting God calm the storms within look like for you?

4

- How has idolatry showed up in your past?
- What forms of idolatry exist in your life right now?
- In what ways is God asking you to take a stronger stand for truth, righteousness, and Godliness?

5

- Which characteristics of the Jezebel spirit have shown up in your life?
- How did those characteristics make you feel?
- Who do you need to ask forgiveness from?
- Who do you need to forgive?

6

- Would you consider yourself spiritually alive in Christ, or have you grown spiritually dead, just going through the motions?
- What does "turning back to God" look like for you?
- What "busywork" have you allowed to overtake you?
- If you're not living the life God ultimately designed for you, what does that look like? What dream has been buried in

your heart and how could you dig it up and use it for God's glory?

- Take some time to journal through the following "Finding My Purpose" questions and ask God for wisdom and discernment as you do.
  - o If I could wake up tomorrow and not worry about any responsibilities or money, what would I do with my life?
  - o What did I dream of doing when I was kid?
  - o What are the things people are always telling me that I am good at, and how do those qualities fit with my dreams?
  - o What do I want my life legacy to be?
  - o Where do I want to travel?
  - o What experiences do I want to have?
  - o How do I really want to be spending my free time?
  - o What would I say and do if I wasn't afraid of what people would think of me?
  - o What are the things that are important to me?
  - o What am I willing to give up so I can live my life authentically?

7

- What are the lies and labels that others have put on you, or that you have put on yourself?
- Would you say you are more afraid of success or of failure? Why?
- How would you describe a fearless woman?
- Think of a situation that you are currently afraid of. How can you display courage in that this week?
- What has God been telling you as you confront your fears?

8

- When you read Revelation 3:8-11, what jumps out at you the most?
- How do you identify with my story of faith and healing?
- What doors has God opened for you that you need to walk through by faith?
- What doors has God closed for you that you need to fully release to him and stop looking back on?
- What characteristics from this passage do you already have in you?
- What is God saying to you right now, in this moment?

9

- In what ways have you forgotten your first love?
- How would you describe Jesus' love for you and your relationship with him?
- Describe a time when his love for you swept you off your feet.
- What verses speak to your heart like personal love letters from Jesus?

10

- Would you describe your relationship with God as hot, cold, or stagnant and stale?
- What did God reveal to you in this chapter?
- In what ways has God brought you through a Refiner's Fire?
- Describe the character, faith, persistence, and courage that is evident in your life right now.
- How can you put on God's wardrobe this week?

- Would you describe your spiritual eyesight as weak, strong, or completely blind?

11

- Do you find expressing gratitude to be an easy or a hard thing for you to do? Why?
- Write down 10 things that you are thankful for today. Keep doing this every day by starting a 30 Day Gratitude Journal.
- In what ways do you need to apply grace to your life this week?
- In what ways do you need to extend grace to others?
- Take some time to journal through the following "Redeemed of Uncertainties" questions and ask God for wisdom and discernment as you do.
    o What are the current "ashes" in your life, and in what ways can you express gratitude in the midst of them? (Chapter One)
    o How can you have a heart of gratitude towards the suffering that you've endured? (Chapter Two)
    o In what ways can you be thankful for the times that you've been weary? (Chapter Three)
    o How has discovering the hidden idols in your life made you more thankful? (Chapter Four)
    o In what ways can you be thankful for the Jezzies in your life? (Chapter Five)
    o When it comes to finding your purpose and living authentically, what are you thankful for? (Chapter Six)
    o In what ways are you thankful for the lies, labels, and fears that you've experienced and overcome? (Chapter Seven)

- What doors has God shut for you that you are thankful for? What doors has He opened that you are thankful for? (Chapter Eight)
- When it comes to remembering your first love, what are you thankful for? (Chapter Nine)
- What refining process have you been through and how has it made you more grateful? (Chapter Ten)

RELATED WORDS OF LIFE ARCHIVE:

"To the angel of the church in Smyrna write: These are the words of him who is the First and the Last, who died and came to life again. I know your afflictions and your poverty—yet you are rich! I know about the slander of those who say they are Jews and are not, but are a synagogue of Satan. Do not be afraid of what you are about to suffer. I tell you, the devil will put some of you in prison to test you, and you will suffer persecution for ten days. Be faithful, even to the point of death, and I will give you life as your victor's crown. Whoever has ears, let them hear what the Spirit says to the churches. The one who is victorious will not be hurt at all by the second death." ~Revelation 2:8-11, NIV*

"And my God will meet all your needs according to his glorious riches in Christ Jesus." ~Philippians 4:19, NIV*

Write this to Smyrna, to the Angel of the church. The Beginning and Ending, the First and Final One, the Once Dead and Then Come Alive, speaks: I can see your pain and poverty—constant pain, dire poverty—but I also see your wealth. And I hear the lie in the claims of those who pretend to be good Jews, who in fact belong to Satan's crowd. Fear nothing in the things you're about to suffer—but stay on guard! Fear nothing! The Devil is about to throw you in jail for a time of testing—ten days. It won't last forever. Don't quit, even if it costs you your life. Stay there believing. I have a Life-Crown sized and ready for you. Are your ears awake? Listen. Listen to the Wind Words, the Spirit blowing through the churches. Christ-conquerors are safe from Devil-death." ~Revelation 2:8-11, MSG*

"We also rejoice in our sufferings, because we know that suffering produces perseverance; perseverance, character; and character, hope. And hope does not disappoint us, because God has poured out his love into our hearts by the Holy Spirit, whom he has given us." ~Romans 5:3-5, NIV

"Consider it a sheer gift, friends, when tests and challenges come at you from all sides. You know that under pressure, your faith-life is forced into the open and shows its true colors. So don't try to get out of anything prematurely. Let it do its work so you become mature and well-developed, not deficient in any way." ~James 1:2-4, *The Message*

"Now faith is being sure of what we hope for, and confident of what we do not see." ~Hebrews 11:1, NIV

"And without faith it is impossible to please God, because anyone who comes to him must believe that he exists and that he rewards those who earnestly seek him." ~Hebrews 11:6, NIV

"Give your entire attention to what God is doing right now, and don't get worked up about what may or may not happen tomorrow. God will help you deal with whatever hard things come up when the time comes." ~Matthew 6:34, *The Message*

"Come to me, all you who are weary and burdened, and I will give you rest." ~Matthew 11:28, NIV

"For I have given rest to the weary and joy to the sorrowing." ~Jeremiah 31:25, NLT

"So we see that because of their unbelief they were not able to enter his rest." ~Hebrews 3:19, NLT

"There remains, then, a Sabbath rest for the people of God." ~Hebrews 4:9, NIV

"To the angel of the church in Pergamum write: These are the words of him who has the sharp, double-edged sword. I know where you live—where Satan has his throne. Yet you remain true to my name. You did not renounce your faith in me, not even in the days of Antipas, my faithful witness, who was put to death in your city—where Satan lives. Nevertheless, I have a few things against you: There are some among you who hold to the teaching of Balaam, who taught Balak to entice the Israelites to sin so that they ate food sacrificed to idols and committed sexual immorality. Likewise, you also have those who hold to the teaching of the Nicolaitans. Repent therefore! Otherwise, I will soon come to you and will fight against them with the sword of my mouth. Whoever has ears, let them hear what the Spirit says to the churches. To the one who is victorious, I will give some of the hidden manna. I will also give that person a white stone with a new name written on it, known only to the one who receives it." ~Revelation 2:12-17, NIV

"Write this to Pergamum, to the Angel of the church. The One with the sharp-biting sword draws from the sheath of his mouth—out come the sword words: I see where you live, right under the shadow of Satan's throne. But you continue boldly in my Name; you never once denied my Name, even when the pressure was worst, when they martyred Antipas, my witness who stayed faithful to me on Satan's turf. But why do you indulge that Balaam crowd? Don't you remember that Balaam was an enemy agent, seducing Balak and sabotaging Israel's holy pilgrimage by throwing unholy parties? And why

do you put up with the Nicolaitans, who do the same thing? Enough! Don't give in to them; I'll be with you soon. I'm fed up and about to cut them to pieces with my sword-sharp words. Are your ears awake? Listen. Listen to the Wind Words, the Spirit blowing through the churches. I'll give the sacred manna to every conqueror; I'll also give a clear, smooth stone inscribed with your new name, your secret new name." ~Revelation 2:12-17, *The Message*

"You shall have no other gods before me." ~Exodus 20:3

"Blessed is the one who does not walk in step with the wicked or stand in the way that sinners take or sit in the company of mockers, but whose delight is in the law of the Lord, and who meditates on his law day and night." ~Psalm 1:1-2

"Some trust in chariots and some in horses, but we trust in the name of the Lord our God. They are brought to their knees and fall, but we rise up and stand firm." ~Psalm 20:7-8

"But we do not belong to those who shrink back and are destroyed, but to those who have faith and are saved." ~Hebrews 10:39

"So do not throw away your confidence; it will be richly rewarded. You need to persevere so that when you have done the will of God, you will receive what he has promised." ~Hebrews 10:35

"I urge you, brothers and sisters, to watch out for those who cause divisions and put obstacles in your way that are contrary to the teaching you have learned. Keep away from them. 18 For such people are not serving our Lord Christ, but their own appetites. By smooth talk and flattery they deceive the minds of naive people." ~Romans 16:17-18

"My son, pay attention to what I say; turn your ear to my words. Do not let them out of your sight, keep them within your heart; for they are life to those who find them and health to one's whole body. Above all else, guard your heart, for everything you do flows from it." ~Proverbs 4:20-23

"Therefore, if anyone is in Christ, the new creation has come: The old has gone, the new is here!" ~1 Corinthians 5:17

"So if the Son sets you free, you will be free indeed." ~John 8:36

"These are the words of the Son of God, whose eyes are like blazing fire and whose feet are like burnished bronze. I know your deeds, your love and faith, your service and perseverance, and that you are now doing more than you did at first. Nevertheless, I have this against you: You tolerate that woman Jezebel, who calls herself a prophetess. By her teaching she misleads my servants into sexual immorality and the eating of food sacrificed to idols. I have given her time to repent of her immorality, but she is unwilling. So I will cast her on a bed of suffering, and I will make those who commit adultery with her suffer intensely, unless they repent of her ways. I will strike her children dead. Then all the churches will know that I am he who searches hearts and minds, and I will repay each of you according to your deeds. Now I say to the rest of you in Thyatira, to you who do not hold to her teaching and have not learned Satan's so-called deep secrets (I will not impose any other burden on you): Only hold on to what you have until I come. To him who overcomes and does my will to the end, I will give authority over the nations –'He will rule them with an iron scepter; he will dash them to pieces like pottery' – just as I have received authority from my Father. I will also give him the morning star. He who has an

ear, let him hear what the Spirit says to the churches."
~Revelation 2:18-29

"There was never a man like Ahab, who sold himself to do evil in the eyes of the Lord, urged on by Jezebel his wife. He behaved in the vilest manner by going after idols," ~1 Kings 21:25-26 NIV

"The Lord does not look at the things people look at. People look at the outward appearance, but the Lord looks at the heart." ~1 Samuel 16:7 NIV

"Therefore, there is now no condemnation for those who are in Christ Jesus." ~Romans 8:1

"Then every church will know that appearances don't impress me. I x-ray every motive." ~Revelation 2:23, *The Message*

"Don't copy the behavior and customs of this world, but let God transform you into a new person by changing the way you think. Then you will learn to know God's will for you, which is good and pleasing and perfect." ~Romans 12:2 NLT

"Up on your feet! Take a deep breath! Maybe there's life in you yet. But I wouldn't know it by looking at your busywork; nothing of GOD's work has been completed. Your condition is desperate. Think of the gift you once had in your hands, the Message you heard with your ears – grasp it again and turn back to God. If you pull the covers back over your head and sleep on, oblivious to God, I'll return when you least expect it, break into your life like a thief in the night. You still have a few followers of Jesus in Sardis who haven't ruined themselves wallowing in the muck of the world's ways. They'll walk with me on parade! They've proved their worth! Conquerors will march in the victory parade, their names indelible in the Book of Life. I'll lead them up and present them by name to my

Father and his Angels. Are your ears awake? Listen. Listen to the Wind Words, the Spirit blowing through the churches."
~Revelation 3:1-6, *The Message*

"When God lives and breathes in you (and he does, as surely as he did in Jesus), you are delivered from that dead life."
~Romans 8:11, *The Message*

"Therefore, if anyone is in Christ, he is a new creation; the old has gone, the new has come!" ~2 Corinthians 5:17, NIV

"For we are God's workmanship, created in Christ Jesus to do good works, which God prepared in advance for us to do."
~Ephesians 2:10, NIV

"But because of his great love for us, God, who is rich in mercy, made us alive with Christ even when we were dead in transgressions-it is by grace you have been saved."
~Ephesians 2:4-5, NIV

"Be joyful always; pray continually; give thanks in all circumstances, for this is God's will for you in Christ Jesus."
~1 Thessalonians 5:16-18, NIV

"For I know the plans I have for you, declares the Lord, plans to prosper you and not to harm you, plans to give you hope and a future." ~Jeremiah 29:11, NIV

"She will have no fear of bad news; her heart is steadfast, trusting in the Lord. Her heart is secure, she will have no fear; in the end she will look in triumph on her foes." ~Psalm 112:7-8

"I have given you authority to trample on snakes and scorpions and to overcome all the power of the enemy; nothing will harm you." ~Luke 10:19

"But he said to me, 'My grace is sufficient for you, for my power is made perfect in weakness.' Therefore I will boast all the more gladly about my weaknesses, so that Christ's power may rest on me. That is why, for Christ's sake, I delight in weaknesses, in insults, in hardships, in persecutions, in difficulties. For when I am weak, then I am strong." ~2 Corinthians 12:9-10, NIV

"Even though I walk through the darkest valley, I will fear no evil, for you are with me; your rod and your staff, they comfort me." ~Psalm 23:4, NIV

"For I am the Lord your God who takes hold of your right hand and says to you, Do not fear; I will help you." ~Isaiah 41:13, NIV

"Moses answered the people, "Do not be afraid. Stand firm and you will see the deliverance the Lord will bring you today." ~Exodus 14:13, NIV

"Be strong and courageous. Do not be afraid or terrified because of them, for the Lord your God goes with you; he will never leave you nor forsake you." ~Deuteronomy 31:6, NIV

"For the Spirit God gave us does not make us timid, but gives us power, love and self-discipline." ~2 Timothy 1:7, NIV

"The Lord is my light and my salvation—whom shall I fear? The Lord is the stronghold of my life—of whom shall I be afraid?" ~Psalm 27:1, NIV

"So we say with confidence, "The Lord is my helper; I will not be afraid. What can mere mortals do to me?" ~Hebrews 13:6, NIV

"Peace I leave with you; my peace I give you. I do not give to you as the world gives. Do not let your hearts be troubled and do not be afraid." ~John 14:27, NIV

"I see what you've done. Now see what I've done. I've opened a door before you that no one can slam shut. You don't have much strength, I know that; you used what you had to keep my Word. You didn't deny me when times were rough. And watch as I take those who call themselves true believers but are nothing of the kind, pretenders whose true membership is in the club of Satan – watch as I strip off their pretensions and they're forced to acknowledge it's you that I've loved. Because you kept my Word in passionate patience, I'll keep you safe in the time of testing that will be here soon, and all over the earth, every man, woman, and child put to the test. I'm on my way; I'll be there soon. Keep a tight grip on what you have so no one distracts you and steals your crown." ~Revelation 3:8-11, *The Message*

"May the God of hope fill you with all joy and peace as you trust in him, so that you may overflow with hope by the power of the Holy Spirit." ~Romans 15:13, NIV

"So let God work his will in you. Yell a loud no to the Devil and watch him scamper. Say a quiet yes to God and he'll be there in no time. Quit dabbling in sin. Purify your inner life. Quit playing the field. Hit bottom, and cry your eyes out. The fun and games are over. Get serious, really serious. Get down on your knees before your Master; it's the only way you'll get on your feet." ~James 4:7-10, *The Message*

"Forget the former things; do not dwell on the past. See, I am doing a new thing! Now it springs up; do you not perceive it? I am making a way in the desert and streams in the wasteland." ~Isaiah 43:18-19, NIV

"Now faith is confidence in what we hope for and assurance about what we do not see." ~Hebrews 11:1, NLT

"I see what you've done, your hard, hard work, your refusal to quit. I know you can't stomach evil, that you weed out apostolic pretenders. I know your persistence, your courage in my cause, that you never wear out. But you walked away from your first love—why? What's going on with you, anyway? Do you have any idea how far you've fallen? A Lucifer fall! Turn back! Recover your dear early love. No time to waste, for I'm well on my way to removing your light from the golden circle. You do have this to your credit: You hate the Nicolaitan business. I hate it, too. Are your ears awake? Listen. Listen to the Wind Words, the Spirit blowing through the churches. I'm about to call each conqueror to dinner. I'm spreading a banquet of Tree-of-Life fruit, a supper plucked from God's orchard." ~Revelation 2:2-7, *The Message*

"Therefore, since we are surrounded by such a great cloud of witnesses, let us throw off everything that hinders and the sin that so easily entangles. And let us run with perseverance the race marked out for us, ² fixing our eyes on Jesus, the pioneer and perfecter of faith. For the joy set before him he endured the cross, scorning its shame, and sat down at the right hand of the throne of God." ~Hebrews 12:1-2, NIV

"Restore to me the joy of your salvation and grant me a willing spirit, to sustain me." ~Psalm 51:12, NIV

"For God so loved the world that he gave his one and only Son, that whoever believes in him shall not perish but have eternal life." ~John 3:16, NIV

"keep yourselves in God's love as you wait for the mercy of our Lord Jesus Christ to bring you to eternal life." ~Jude 1:21, NIV

"I know you inside and out, and find little to my liking. You're

not cold, you're not hot—far better to be either cold or hot! You're stale. You're stagnant. You make me want to vomit. You brag, 'I'm rich, I've got it made, I need nothing from anyone,' oblivious that in fact you're a pitiful, blind beggar, threadbare and homeless. Here's what I want you to do: Buy your gold from me, gold that's been through the refiner's fire. Then you'll be rich. Buy your clothes from me, clothes designed in Heaven. You've gone around half-naked long enough. And buy medicine for your eyes from me so you can see, really see. The people I love, I call to account—prod and correct and guide so that they'll live at their best. Up on your feet, then! About face! Run after God! Look at me. I stand at the door. I knock. If you hear me call and open the door, I'll come right in and sit down to supper with you. Conquerors will sit alongside me at the head table, just as I, having conquered, took the place of honor at the side of my Father. That's my gift to the conquerors!" ~Revelation 3:15-21, *The Message*

"Be prepared. You're up against far more than you can handle on your own. Take all the help you can get, every weapon God has issued, so that when it's all over but the shouting you'll still be on your feet. Truth, righteousness, peace, faith, and salvation are more than words. Learn how to apply them. You'll need them throughout your life. God's Word is an indispensable weapon. In the same way, prayer is essential in this ongoing warfare. Pray hard and long. Pray for your brothers and sisters. Keep your eyes open. Keep each other's spirits up so that no one falls behind or drops out." ~Ephesians 6:10-18, *The Message*

"The night is almost gone, and the day is near. Therefore let us lay aside the deeds of darkness and put on the armor of light." ~ Romans 13:12

"So, as those who have been chosen of God, holy and beloved, put on a heart of compassion, kindness, humility, gentleness and patience." ~ Colossians 3:12

"You younger men, likewise, be subject to your elders; and all of you, clothe yourselves with humility toward one another, for God is opposed to the proud, but gives grace to the humble." ~ 1 Peter 5:5

"So, as those who have been chosen of God, holy and beloved, put on a heart of compassion, kindness, humility, gentleness and patience; bearing with one another, and forgiving each other, whoever has a complaint against anyone; just as the Lord forgave you, so also should you. Beyond all these things put on love, which is the perfect bond of unity." ~ Colossians 3:12-14

"Put on the full armor of God, so that you will be able to stand firm against the schemes of the devil. For our struggle is not against flesh and blood, but against the rulers, against the powers, against the world forces of this darkness, against the spiritual forces of wickedness in the heavenly places. Therefore, take up the full armor of God, so that you will be able to resist in the evil day, and having done everything, to stand firm. Stand firm therefore, having girded your loins with truth, and having put on the breastplate of righteousness, and having shod your feet with the preparation of the gospel of peace; in addition to all, taking up the shield of faith with which you will be able to extinguish all the flaming arrows of the evil one. And take THE HELMET OF SALVATION, and the sword of the Spirit, which is the word of God. With all prayer and petition pray at all times in the Spirit, and with this in view, be on the alert with all perseverance and petition for all the saints." ~ Ephesians 6:11-18

"He will sit as a refiner and purifier of silver; he will purify the Levites and refine them like gold and silver. Then the LORD will have men who will bring offerings in righteousness..."
~Malachi 3:3, NIV

"Rejoice always, pray continually, give thanks in all circumstances; for this is God's will for you in Christ Jesus."
~1 Thessalonians 5:16-18, NIV

"See to it that no one falls short of the grace of God and that no bitter root grows up to cause trouble and defile many."
~Hebrews 12:15, NIV

"And the God of all grace, who called you to his eternal glory in Christ, after you have suffered a little while, will himself restore you and make you strong, firm and steadfast." ~1 Peter 5:10, NIV

"The Spirit of the Sovereign LORD is on me, because the LORD has anointed me to preach good news to the poor. He has sent me to bind up the brokenhearted, to proclaim freedom for the captives and release from darkness for the prisoners, 2 to proclaim the year of the LORD's favor and the day of vengeance of our God, to comfort all who mourn, 3 and provide for those who grieve in Zion-- to bestow on them a crown of beauty instead of ashes, the oil of gladness instead of mourning, and a garment of praise instead of a spirit of despair. They will be called oaks of righteousness, a planting of the LORD for the display of his splendor." ~Isaiah 61:1-3, NIV

ABOUT THE AUTHOR

Mandy B. Anderson is a Leadership Coach, Author, Keynote Speaker, and the Co-Founder of RAYMA Team. She helps women embrace the qualities they need to be healthy and live their lives with intention. Anderson vulnerably shares her story of living with Cystic Fibrosis, and overcoming deep losses and mistakes in life, to encourage others to courageously live their lives to the fullest no matter what they face.

Mandy is a Certified Life Coach, a Certified L.E.A.N. Health Coach, an upcoming TEDx Speaker, and was awarded the honor of being in the Top 25 Women in Business for 2020 by Prairie Business Magazine. She lives by the water in North Dakota with her husband, Nate, where she sips her coffee every morning and watches the sunrise with a smile on her face. Read her blogs about life with cystic fibrosis at www.mandybanderson.com.

***

OTHER BOOKS BY MANDY B. ANDERSON

In Sickness and In Health: Lessons Learned on the Journey from Cystic Fibrosis to Total Health

She Cultivates Resilience: 7 Principles to Step into the Shoes of a Resilient Woman (Anderson & Perman)

SUBSCRIBE TO THE SHE WHO OVERCOMES PODCAST

Hosted by RAYMA Team Co-Founders, Mandy B. Anderson & Raychel Perman, the She Who Overcomes™ Podcast is a series of real-life stories and conversations that provides the listener with hope and action steps to transform your life, leadership, and career. Listen and subscribe on Apple Podcast. New episodes drop every Monday!

ABOUT RAYMA TEAM, LLC

RAYMA Team, LLC is a woman owned business that equips women with leadership skills to overcome obstacles in their life and career. Owners, Mandy B. Anderson and Raychel Perman, are two besties on a mission dedicated to equipping other women to rise up, lead well, and live with intention. They offer group coaching programs, leadership and workplace training, private coaching, speaking services, as well as books and free resources on their website at www.raymateam.com.

CPSIA information can be obtained
at www.ICGtesting.com
Printed in the USA
BVHW040407300321
603640BV00002B/102